"I'm excited about ~~Bob~~ *Letter Prayer Life*. He shows how just seventeen ~~words~~ ~~ph~~rases of Jesus impart the secrets of prayer—the fountain and source of a thousand blessings. This is a book to be read and reread."

    -Josh McDowell, author of *More Than a Carpenter*

"Red Letter in the title refers the prayers of Jesus, printed in red in some translations. Hostetler's book builds on the request of the first disciples, 'Lord, teach us to pray.' For those who want to develop a committed, disciplined prayer life, the author takes them through simple, direct instructions. The poignant stories he uses to illustrate the steps warm the heart."

    - Cecil Murphey, author or co-author of more than 130 books including *90 Minutes in Heaven* with Don Piper and *Gifted Hands: The Ben Carson Story*

"Bob Hostetler has created one of the most genuinely satisfying and cordial books about prayer for Christians that I have ever seen. It is engaging, humble, and totally appealing, while at the same time being deeply scriptural. I rejoice in this book and can only hope many others will too."

    - Phyllis Tickle, compiler, THE DIVINE HOURS

"Bob Hostetler writes about prayer with the enthusiasm and experience of someone who has immersed himself in the subject. Nothing here feels second-hand but lived, tried and tested. This book will expand your prayer life. It did mine."

    - Rick Hamlin, executive editor, *Guideposts* magazine

"No matter what level of prayer life you have—from almost none to a good one—*The Red Letter Prayer Life* will encourage and challenge you to go deeper. I highly recommend it."

- Jonathan Graf, publisher, *Prayer Connect* magazine

"Bob Hostetler's marvelous sense of humor is so fresh, witty, and spontaneous, it is only later, upon reflection, that readers realize they have been taught profound lessons while being thoroughly entertained. Bob is optimistic but not naïve. He's motivating without being demanding. He's corrective while also empathetic. Read this book slowly and savor its nurturing."

-Dr. Dennis E. Hensley, author of *Jesus in the 9 to 5*

"*The Red Letter Prayer Life* is superb. Not only does Bob Hostetler walk the reader through the variants of prayer. . . but he also guides the reader to drop the walls of formality and come to the feet of God openly and with passion. This book is a must for anyone wishing to deepen a personal relationship with Christ through prayer."

- Cindy K. Sproles, author and cofounder of Christian Devotions Ministries

"Bob Hostetler shows in *The Red Letter Prayer Life* marvelous ways we can enjoy God's presence through prayer. Using stories and analogies, Bob explains how to be enriched in our times of prayer while reading what Jesus taught in The Lord's Prayer. I highly recommend *The Red Letter Prayer Life* to anyone searching for a richer experience with Jesus."

- Anita Corrine Donihue, author of When I'm on My Knees Series and other titles, two million–plus copies sold

The RED
LETTER
Prayer Life

The RED LETTER
Prayer Life

17 **Words** from **Jesus** to Inspire Practical, Purposeful, Powerful **Prayer**

BOB HOSTETLER

SHILOH RUN  PRESS

An Imprint of Barbour Publishing, Inc.

Dedicated to Avery, Ryder, Calleigh, Mia, and Miles.

May your lives be shaped and marked and enriched by prayer, and may you "pray in the Spirit on all occasions with all kinds of prayers and requests" (Ephesians 6:18 NIV).

Print ISBN 978-1-63058-851-9

eBook Editions:
Adobe Digital Edition (.epub) 978-1-63409-292-0
Kindle and MobiPocket Edition (.prc) 978-1-63409-293-7

Cover design by Kirk DouPonce, DogEared Design

Published by Shiloh Run Press, an imprint of Barbour Publishing, Inc., P.O. Box 719, Uhrichsville, Ohio 44683, www.shilohrunpress.com

Our mission is to publish and distribute inspirational products offering exceptional value and biblical encouragement to the masses.

Member of the
Evangelical Christian
Publishers Association

Printed in the United States of America.

ACKNOWLEDGMENTS

Thank you to my agent and friend, Steve Laube of the Steve Laube Agency, for representing me on this project.

Thank you to Kelly McIntosh and Barbour Publishing for the vision, constant professionalism, and Christlike values that make them such a pleasure to work with from beginning to end.

Thank you to my friends Michelle Medlock-Adams, Cindy Sproles, and Greg Stier for giving me permission to share their prayer experiences.

Thank you to my prayer partners who supported me and this project in prayer: Darryl Handy, Dewey Hughes, Suzan Hughes, Cheryl Johnson, Bill Riley, Debbie Stacy, Doug Webb, Julie Webb, Jane Wright, and the prayer ministry at Cincinnati's Vineyard Community Church. Your ministry to me and to the readers of this book is deeply appreciated.

Thank you to those who have formed and influenced and enriched my prayer life over many years (many of whom should be obvious from being quoted or mentioned in these pages): Andrew Murray, Thomas Merton, Peter Marshall, John Baillie, Henri Nouwen, Eugene Peterson, the Reverend Dr. Chip Lee, Phyllis Tickle, and the monks (past and present) of the Abbey of Gethsemani.

Thank you also and most of all to the lovely Robin, my wife, whose patience, kindness, encouragement, support, and approval mean more to me than words can express.

CONTENTS

1

The Riches of the Red Letter Prayer Life

—

I want to fly first class.

Go ahead, judge me. I don't fly as much as some people do, but I log many thousands of air travel miles every year. And I'm not the only one to notice that sitting space on planes seems to be shrinking and comfort is disappearing. Have you ever had a leg cramp while seated in a non-exit row in coach? Well, I have, and while I'm sure it doesn't compare to childbirth or a kidney stone, it's no picnic at the beach, let me tell you.

In all my years of air travel—and I started flying just after the Wright brothers—I have had a first-class seat only once, and that was an unexpected upgrade. I can't remember how it happened, but I didn't turn it down. It gave me a glimpse into all the blessings I'd been missing: legroom, armrests all to myself, a free newspaper, hot hand towels, actual silverware, and more. I would have felt like the king of Siam except I think he was sitting across the aisle from me.

So, yes, I want to fly first class again. Someday, at least. Whenever possible. It's not just about comfort for me; it's also about luxury.

I think most of us want to fly first class. We want to be comfortable. We would even welcome a little luxury. It would be nice. To coin a phrase (or more precisely, to use a phrase that has been coined and spent many times), it would be "a blessing."

We want a blessed life. And while some of that desire for blessing can be sinful, even idolatrous (if it translates into such things as consumerism or instant gratification, as I wrote about in my book *American Idols*), it can also be understandable, even righteous. There's nothing wrong with preferring the first-class cabin to the nonreclining last row on the plane. There's nothing wrong with enjoying a great meal or a good book. There's nothing wrong with dressing well and traveling widely. No less an expert than wise King Solomon said:

> *Seize life! Eat bread with gusto,*
> *Drink wine with a robust heart.*
> *Oh yes—God takes pleasure in your pleasure!*
> *Dress festively every morning.*
> *Don't skimp on colors and scarves.*
> *Relish life with the spouse you love*
> *Each and every day of your precarious life.*
> *Each day is God's gift. It's all you get in exchange*
> *For the hard work of staying alive.*
> *Make the most of each one!*
> *Whatever turns up, grab it and do it. And heartily!*[1]

We shouldn't be selfish, of course, but we can admit to craving the best things this world and this life have to offer. Even our first parents, Adam and Eve, must have craved and consumed a lot of good fruit—with no ill effects—before they eventually sank their teeth into one bad apple, so to speak. And it's not only material comforts we long for but also intangible things. Who wouldn't like more confidence at times? Who wouldn't welcome more time and more strength? Who doesn't need a little more peace? And patience? And laughter, and love, and beauty? Talk about a blessed life! Where do we sign up? How do we qualify? What does it take?

SOME SOURCES ARE BETTER THAN OTHERS

Years ago, when my two children were in grade school (they're almost as old as me now), I took them on occasional backpacking trips in the Smoky Mountains of Tennessee, one of my favorite spots on earth. I would map out our route on a trail map, usually choosing a scenic spot such as a waterfall for our destination. We would each carry our own bed, food, book (always a book), and other necessities in our packs. We would hike for a few hours each day and then set up camp, play, cook, read, and relax until the sun went down. On most trips we hiked two days in and two days back before heading home.

Those were precious times. I enjoyed not only the many hours of closeness with my kids but also imparting some spiritual insights and a little trail of wisdom to them. They learned how to pack wisely and how to make and break camp well. They learned to carve a willow whistle and cook over a campfire. They learned how much better food tastes on the trail. They learned to dig a latrine and purify drinking water.

On one backpacking trip, however, we all became a little lax in our water purification efforts. By "a little lax," I mean "completely neglected it." We drank the cool, clear water straight from the stream along which we hiked. For mile after mile, we didn't boil or filter our water. We didn't use purification tablets either. And we suffered no consequences. Everything was peachy. Until we reached our destination.

We took our time hiking through the sylvan scenery along Abrams Creek, seldom losing sight of the stream as we followed the moderate trail. We could hear the thunder of the low falls before they came into view, and then a footbridge allowed us to keep our feet dry as we crossed Wilson Branch. A moment later, we arrived and saw not only the beautiful waterfall but also the broad pool at its base. . .where a dozen or so people not only waded and swam but even stood shampooing their hair!

The kids and I exchanged glances. No words were necessary. Our foolishness was too obvious. For two full days we had been drinking unpurified water from a contaminated source.

That was the last time we did that, because you can't get clean water from a nasty source. You can't draw pure things out of something impure. As Jesus said, "A healthy tree cannot bear bad fruit, nor can a diseased tree bear good fruit."[2]

It's a pretty fundamental principle. But we ignore it all the time. We look for good stuff in bad places. We try to build the good life out of bad materials. We want blessed lives, but we try to cobble them together ourselves rather than seeking them from what hymn writer Basil Wood called the "source of every blessing."[3]

THE MOST BLESSED LIFE

If anyone exemplifies the blessed life, it is Jesus. Though He never owned a home or car and never held season tickets for His favorite baseball team (the Cincinnati Reds, in case you were wondering), He lived a singular life. A rich life. A healing life. A life filled with laughter and song. A life that exuded beauty and blessing.

If you read the Gospels—Matthew, Mark, Luke, and John—carefully, you'll see the portrait of a man who commanded the very elements of earth and sky, wind and wave, to do His bidding. He was supremely confident and at ease, whether He was in the presence of a leper or a Roman governor. He was uncowed by demons. He was unfazed by storms. He was the quintessential "blessed man" of David's psalm:

Blessed is the man
who walks not in the counsel of the wicked,
nor stands in the way of sinners,
*   nor sits in the seat of scoffers;*
but his delight is in the law of the LORD,
*   and on his law he meditates day and night.*

He is like a tree
*   planted by streams of water*
that yields its fruit in its season,
*   and its leaf does not wither.*
In all that he does, he prospers.[4]

His life was the epitome of Balaam's Spirit-inspired prophecy concerning the people of Israel:

"Like palm groves that stretch out,
*   like gardens next to a river,*
*   like eaglewood trees that the LORD has planted,*
*   like cedar trees next to water.*
Water will drip from his branches;
*   his seed will have plenty of water."*[5]

Jesus could have been the poster boy for Jeremiah's depiction of the blessed life:

> *"Blessed is the man who trusts in the LORD,*
> *whose trust is the LORD.*
> *He is like a tree planted by water,*
> *that sends out its roots by the stream,*
> *and does not fear when heat comes,*
> *for its leaves remain green,*
> *and is not anxious in the year of drought,*
> *for it does not cease to bear fruit."* 6

He could endure intense temptation without giving in. He could withstand violent opposition without buckling. He could sleep through a storm. He could heal with a touch or a word. He could charm children and mesmerize crowds. He knew how to work hard, and He knew how to rest well. He owed nothing and owned little but never wanted. He constantly gave but never suffered the least diminution.

Imagine a life like that. A blessed life. The richest life there could ever be.

But how did Jesus live such a life? How did He get those riches? Was He born to such blessing? Did He bring those things with Him from heaven? Were such blessings His because He was the Christ, the Anointed One, the Messiah? Or did He access those blessings in the same way we can?

THE MORE BLESSED LIFE

As blessed as Jesus' life on earth was, He told His followers that they couldn't enjoy the same blessings He did; they could enjoy more! He not only said, "Peace I leave with you; my peace I give to you"[7] and "I have given you authority to tread on serpents and scorpions, and over all the power of the enemy, and nothing shall hurt you,"[8] but also said, "Anyone who believes in me will do the same works I have done, and even greater works."[9]

Those words seem to mock us. They sure don't seem to reflect reality. Who among us is enjoying the kind of peace and authority Jesus displayed in His life? Who of us is doing greater things than He did? There is clearly some disconnect between His words and our reality.

I think that's because we've missed something key, something important, something absolutely crucial. I think the snapshots of Jesus we see in the Gospels show us exactly how He—who was thoroughly human in every respect, yet without sin[10]—managed to live the kind of life He did. I think when Jesus bequeathed to Peter "the keys of the kingdom of heaven," so that "whatever you bind on earth shall be bound in heaven, and whatever you loose on earth shall be loosed in heaven,"[11] He referred to keys that are available to all of His followers. And I think at least one of those keys is repeatedly mentioned in no uncertain terms in the accounts of Jesus' life and ministry on earth:

And rising very early in the morning, while it was still dark, he departed and went out to a desolate place, and there he prayed.[12]

And after he had taken leave of them, he went up on the mountain to pray.[13]

But Jesus often withdrew to the wilderness for prayer.[14]

At about that same time he climbed a mountain to pray. He was there all night in prayer before God.[15]

Now it happened that as he was praying alone, the disciples were with him.[16]

And he withdrew from them about a stone's throw, and knelt down and prayed.[17]

Keep in mind, those lines are drawn from first-century accounts of Jesus' life, death, and resurrection, written by men and to people who would have assumed that any observant Jew—let alone a rabbi—would have prayed at least three times a day. And yet the Gospel writers made a point to mention Jesus' frequent prayer retreats. Why?

Because it is necessary to notice His prayer life if we are to understand His blessed life. Prayer was critical to Jesus. It was essential to His connection with the Father. It was vital to the water-to-wine, walking-on-water, lunch-for-the-multitude, and victory-over-sin-and-death kind of life He lived. It was the source of His ability to speak like no one else, before or since. It was the conduit by which He healed the sick, cast out demons, and raised the dead.

That was probably why the earliest followers of Jesus came to Him one day and asked, "Lord, teach us to pray."[18] They weren't saying they had never seen anyone pray before. They'd seen their parents pray. They'd seen priests pray. They'd seen rabbis pray. They also weren't saying they never prayed themselves. They were Jews, after all. They had prayed all their lives. They prayed every morning as soon as they awoke. They said a prayer as they dressed. They prayed before leaving the house. They prayed the Shema three times daily. They probably prayed the Birchot HaShachar—the "eighteen blessings"— every day of their lives.

I think Jesus' first followers asked Him, "Lord, teach us to pray," not because they knew nothing about prayer but because they saw the fruits of His prayer. They discerned that to Jesus, prayer was "the root, the fountain, the mother of a thousand blessings."[19] They recognized that His connection to His Father was key to His enjoyment of life, command of the elements, authority over sickness and Satan, and more. They understood—because they saw it proved in Jesus' life—that "to pray well is to do all things well."[20]

And Jesus answered their request. He taught them to pray. He gave them the keys. He instructed them in prayer that would make the lame walk, open prison doors, and break down barriers between people all over the world. He did it for them, and He did it for you.

"This is what we need to be taught," wrote Andrew Murray. "Though in its beginnings prayer is so simple that the feeble child can pray, yet it is at the same time the highest and holiest work to which [we] can rise. It is fellowship with the Unseen and Most Holy One. The powers of the eternal world have been placed at its disposal. It is the very essence of true religion, the channel of all blessings, the secret of power and life."[21]

That is the goal of the pages that follow—to install in your life the root, the fountain, the channel of a thousand blessings through the words of Jesus on prayer. Each chapter will focus on a single word or phrase from the teachings and prayers of Jesus—the "red letters" of some Bible versions—and help you begin to fashion a red-letter prayer life that will open wide "the channel of all blessings" and unlock "the secret of power and life" for you.

Lord, teach me to pray. Like You. Through You.
With You. In You.
Teach me to want to pray. Teach me to love to pray.
Teach me to seek the fellowship of the Unseen and
Most Holy One, to find solace and strength, power and
pleasure, in prayer.
Teach me to grasp all that is placed at my disposal.
Teach me the very essence of true religion, the channel of
all blessings, the secret of power and life. Amen.

2

PRAY PRIVATELY

—

I was young.

Let's just go with that.

I was no more than twenty years old. I had been married for less than a year. I had no training or experience in home maintenance or kitchen repairs. But I was smart enough to know that drains are supposed to drain and the kitchen sink in the house we rented for $125 a month had filled with water.

I tried pouring Drano down the drain. Didn't work.

I tried Liquid Plumber. That didn't work either.

So more drastic measures were called for. You know what's coming, don't you?

Yes, I calculated that an unfolded wire coat hanger could be plunged into the drain and moved around to dislodge all sorts of drain-plugging materials. I discovered, however, that a wire coat hanger could also pierce an old U-joint as if it had been designed and sharpened for that very purpose.

I tried to convince my wife that, having located the problem, I could successfully replace the faulty U-joint and all would be well. She didn't buy it. We called a plumber.

I've learned a lot since then. And one of the things I've learned is this: When you want to learn how to do something, it's always a good idea to consult someone who has successfully done it. Preferably someone who has successfully done it many times. And even more preferably, someone who does it so well that he or she makes it look easy.

We do it all the time. "How did you do that?" "What's your secret?" "Can you show me?"

Whether it's losing weight. or playing the guitar or throwing a curveball, most of us are smart enough to at least consult an expert when taking on new tasks or learning new skills—or even taking an existing skill to a new level.

That is what the first followers of Jesus did when they came to Him and asked, "Lord, teach us to pray."[1] It was not because they had never prayed but because they saw Him doing it either differently or with better results. Or both. On that occasion—according to Luke, one of Jesus' earliest biographers—He responded with what we have come to call the Lord's Prayer (which we will get to in a few chapters). But that was just one time. Jesus' example of prayer and instruction on prayer pervaded His life and teaching. In fact, early in the Sermon on the Mount—what some scholars believe comprised the mishnah[2] of Rabbi Jesus, the summary of his teachings presented in a format conducive to memorization and repetition—Jesus gave a short lesson in what we might call the red-letter prayer life:

"When you pray, you must not be like the hypocrites.
For they love to stand and pray in the synagogues and
at the street corners, that they may be seen by others.
Truly, I say to you, they have received their reward.
But when you pray, go into your room and shut the
door and pray to your Father who is in secret.
And your Father who sees in secret will reward you."[3]

That is a mere snippet of what Jesus taught about prayer. It is probably among His earliest teachings, but it is brief—only seventy-three words in English (just sixty-six in Greek!). But it says a lot about prayer and offers a clear, concise start in the pursuit of a red-letter prayer life.

WHEN YOU PRAY

Everyone prays. Some people say grace at meals. Some recite bedtime prayers. Some pray with beads or knotted ropes. Some pray in Jesus' name and others in the name of the Father, Son, and Holy Spirit. Some pray to Yahweh while others pray to Allah or "the universe." Some pray daily and others pray sporadically. Some pray knowingly; others pray without realizing it, characterizing their practice as sending out "positive energy" into the world around them. I even knew an atheist who occasionally prayed, saying it was a way of more or less hedging his bets.

When Jesus spoke to His contemporaries about prayer, He didn't say, "*If* you pray." He said, "*When* you pray. . ." He assumed that they prayed. Maybe it was because they—or at least the vast majority of them—were Jews, which meant that they prayed (several times a day, in fact). But it also may have been because they were all human, and prayer is a natural instinct to human beings.

We may not always realize when we are praying. In times of disappointment or upheaval, we may cry out, "Why?" or "Why me?" or "Why this?" without a moment's thought of who we are asking. When a pleasant surprise or unexpected blessing comes our way, it's only natural to feel a surge of gratitude arise in our hearts and souls, though we may never consciously identify it as a prayer. Sometimes a single word— *please* or *no*—escapes our lips without our knowing we've made a sound. At other times our prayer may be nothing more articulate than a quick exhale or intake of air, or even a pleading look or a falling tear.

Jesus knew that His first followers prayed, but not like He prayed. They prayed, but not prayers that multiplied a few loaves and fishes into a lunch for thousands. They prayed, but not raise-the-dead prayers. He also knew prayer was their greatest need. As far as we know, Jesus never taught His followers how to preach. But He instructed them in prayer—and not just once but many times. And He did so from the assumption that they—and we—did pray. And that we would listen to and act on His example and teaching. When He said, "When you pray," He communicated His desire for us to reflect His practice and prescription. He intended for us to pursue a red-letter prayer life.

WHAT NOT TO DO

What Not to Wear was a reality television series that ran on various networks from 2003 through 2013. Most episodes featured someone whose friends, coworkers, or relatives decided that he or she needed a fashion makeover. The nominee (usually a female) would be followed and videotaped without her knowledge for two weeks. The hosts of the show, Stacy and Clinton, would review the secret footage and comment candidly on all that was wrong with the nominee's fashion choices. Then the hosts and the person (or people) who made the nomination would meet the nominee and offer five thousand dollars for the purchase of a new wardrobe, but only after the nominee agreed to accept the hosts' advice and shop according to their rules. The nominee would then be brought to New York City for a week of shopping, hairstyling, skin treatments, and makeup instruction, which would, of course, produce an impressive—even life-changing—transformation. The show became an international success, airing not only in the United States and Canada but also in Spain as *¡No Te Lo Pongas!* (*Don't Put It On!*) and in Portugal and Brazil as *Esquadrão da Moda* (*The Fashion Police*). Versions of the show were also produced in Argentina, Colombia, Italy, and Mexico.

Obviously, knowing what not to do can be a key step in learning what to do, whether you're talking about fashion. . .or prayer. So Jesus, in His early and fundamental teaching on the subject of prayer, started with what not to do. He said, "When you pray, you must not be like the hypocrites. For they love to stand and pray in the synagogues and at the street corners, that they may be seen by others."[4]

To us, those words sound like an exaggeration. After all, we seldom see people standing on street corners, praying. But we are not Jews living in first-century Judea or Galilee, as Jesus was and did.

One of my favorite places in the world is Jerusalem, a place where (literally) you can hardly take a step or turn a corner without encountering something of historical, archaeological, or spiritual significance. One such place is the Kotel, or Western Wall, in Jerusalem's Old City. It is the only surviving part of the ancient complex where the temple once stood, so it is a holy place to Jews. Many of the massive stones in the wall have been worn smooth and polished by the touch of worshippers praying there. The cracks between the stones are crammed with tiny wads of paper on which people have written heartfelt prayers. Whether you visit the Kotel at midday or midnight, there are people standing and praying at the wall, men on one side of a partition and women on the other. As they pray, they move their lips and rock back and forth (some more emphatically than others), a process called *davening*, partly in obedience to the command to "love the LORD your God with all your heart and with all your soul and with all your might."[5]

Prayer by the crowd at the Kotel is similar to prayer as devout Jews practiced it in Jesus' day. The most religious among them would daven not only in the synagogues but also in all sorts of public places, particularly at one of the three formally accepted times of prayer—evening, morning, and noon.[6] So Jesus wasn't overstating matters when He referred to people praying "in the synagogues and at the street corners, that they may be seen by others."[7] It was a common practice to His first listeners.

It is a reality in our day and age, too. We don't daven on street corners, of course. But anyone who prays will face many temptations. One such temptation is to try to sound like someone else when we pray—the pastor, perhaps, or Billy Graham. Another is to impress others with our erudition (note: using the word *erudition* is probably an indication of this). James Mulholland wrote:

> *Many of us, especially those raised in religious homes, have learned to pray the prayer of self-righteousness. . . . It is motivated by pride and vanity. When I pray this way I act as if God answers the most impressive prayers. Of course, I'm not really concerned with whether God answers or not.*

The true purpose of such prayer is to impress people rather
than God. This kind of prayer is all about me: Look at me.
Listen to me. Be impressed with me.
   Jesus called this "praying like the hypocrites" because
to pray this way is to perform rather than pray.
The word "hypocrite" comes from the Greek word for
"actor." The prayer of self-righteousness is meaningless
and empty. It is offensive because it isn't prayer at all.
It is playacting.[8]

Jesus said, "When you pray, don't do it for show." As Anne
Lamott puts it, "It's not for display purposes, like plastic sushi
or neon."[9] Strutting prayer is sham prayer.

PRAY PRIVATELY

   Jesus said, "When you pray, go into your room and shut
the door and pray to your Father who is in secret."[10] With
each phrase, He sends His followers further and deeper into
solitude: Go. Enter your room. Shut the door. Pray. In secret.
Word by word, step by step, He leads to perhaps the strongest
and most powerful word in the whole sequence: *secret.* That's
where He says your best praying will be done. In other words,
pray privately.

   In saying this, Jesus didn't suggest you should never pray
with others. He did not prohibit public prayers or corporate
prayers. After all, He promised His followers, "If two of you
agree on earth about anything they ask, it will be done for
them by my Father in heaven."[11]

   What He did intend, however, is put this way by theologian
N. T. Wright:

What you are in private is what you really are. Go into
your inner room and talk to your Father. You don't have
to make a song and dance about it, and indeed the
fewer people that know you're doing it the better. . . .
The point is to do business with God, one to one.[12]

The red-letter prayer life is one of frequent private prayer, like
that offered by Jesus Himself, who "very early in the morning,
while it was still dark. . .departed and went out to a desolate
place, and. . .prayed,"[13] who "went up on the mountain to
pray,"[14] and who "often withdrew to the wilderness for prayer."[15]

So, Jesus says, do likewise. "Find a quiet, secluded place so
you won't be tempted to role-play before God. Just be there
as simply and honestly as you can manage."[16] Withdraw. Get
alone. Pray privately. And let your public persona—and any
corporate praying you may do—be a reflection of your private
prayer life.

Reap the Rewards

Not only did Jesus assume His early listeners and first
followers would pray ("When you pray"), but He also
apparently assumed that sincere, private prayer would bring
rewards. He said, "When you pray, go into your room and
shut the door and pray to your Father who is in secret. And
your Father who sees in secret will reward you."[17]

Notice that Jesus contrasted your rewards with those of
people who pray for show. "The hypocrites. . .love to stand
and pray in the synagogues and at the street corners, that
they may be seen by others. Truly, I say to you, they have
received their reward."[18] In other words, they already have all

that's coming to them—whatever ego strokes they get from showing off, perhaps, or their promotions to new positions in the ecclesiastical hierarchy. They can expect nothing greater and nothing later.

Not so with you, however. Jesus didn't say, "*Maybe* your Father will reward you." He said your Father *will* reward you. And your reward won't be mere ego strokes or human applause. Your reward will come from the Father—from His bounty, His creativity, and His wisdom and love, and in His time.

Andrew Murray wrote:

> *Jesus assures us that secret prayer cannot be fruitless: its blessing will show itself in our life. We have but in secret, alone with God, to entrust our life before men to Him; He will reward us openly; He will see to it that the answer to prayer be made manifest in His blessing upon us. . . . On our part there should be the childlike simplicity of faith, the confidence that our prayer does bring down a blessing. "He that cometh to God must believe that He is a rewarder of them that seek Him." Not on the strong or fervent feeling with which I pray does the blessing of the closet depend, but upon the love and the power of the Father to whom I there entrust my needs. And therefore the Master has but one desire: Remember your Father is, and sees and hears in secret; go there and stay there, and go again from there in confidence: He will recompense. Trust Him for it; depend upon Him: prayer to the Father cannot be vain; He will reward you openly.*[19]

Not only did Jesus' life show us the example of private prayer, but it also displayed the fruits of private prayer. He knew whereof He spoke! The multiplied loaves and fishes, the healing of lepers, the casting out of demons, the walking on water, the raising of the dead, and the victory over temptation all flowed from a life of private prayer.

"The secret of all failures, and of all true successes," wrote author and evangelist Samuel Logan Brengle, "is hidden in the attitude of the soul in its private walk with God."[20] That secret is seen at work in the life of Jesus, and it will be as surely displayed in the red-letter prayer life.

Gracious, loving Father
who sees and hears in secret,
disclose to me the joys of the secret place.
Teach me to pray there, and stay there, and go again
from there in confidence.
Grant me the rewards of the secret place,
first and foremost, the knowledge that
I have been with You,
and You have met with me,
in Jesus' name, amen.

3

PRAY SIMPLY

~

You step into an elevator on the ground floor. One other person—much taller than you—stands against the back wall. You turn as the elevator door closes and find your floor number on the elevator control panel. You press the button for your floor and notice that the button for the penthouse is already lit.

You hear a voice behind you—friendly but in a language you don't understand. You turn, smile, and shrug. You don't want to be rude, but you're feeling uncomfortable.

The other passenger speaks again. You feel yourself blushing. You turn. "I'm sorry, I don't speak your language."

Suddenly the ride to your floor seems unbearably long. Your heart beats faster. Your palms start to sweat. You watch the floor numbers above the door light up, one after the other. When the doors finally open to your floor, you dash out like a human cannonball.

That is something like how prayer feels to some people. Like entering a strange room. Meeting someone new. Being expected to use an unfamiliar language.

It can be daunting. Even frightening. Even if you already know the person in the room, so to speak—even if you have a relationship with God—He can seem intimidating.

But it doesn't have to be that way. It doesn't have to be difficult or complicated. The red-letter prayer life is one that is characterized by simple prayer.

THE SIMPLEST FORM OF SPEECH

We make prayer too complicated. We assume that prayer requires knowledge and expertise, eloquence and education. But Jesus told His first followers to keep it simple:

> *"When you pray, do not heap up empty phrases as the Gentiles do, for they think that they will be heard for their many words. Do not be like them, for your Father knows what you need before you ask him."* [1]

Just as Jesus distinguished the showy prayer of some devout Jews from the private prayer habit He urged on His disciples, He also contrasted the incantations many non-Jews used to get some god or goddess to grant their wishes with the simple prayer that should characterize His followers. He said, in effect, "You don't have to get God's attention. You don't have to wake Him up. You don't have to use the right words. You don't have to get fancy. You don't have to beat your breast or dance a jig."

As hymn writer James Montgomery wrote:

> *Prayer is the simplest form of speech*
> *That infant lips can try.* [2]

In other words, keep it sweet and simple because, as Jesus said, "your Father knows what you need before you ask him." [3] According to Jesus, that fact is a fundamental of the red-letter prayer life. It ought to form the basis of why and how you pray.

LET GO OF THE NEED TO "GET IT RIGHT"

If "your Father knows what you need before you ask him," you don't need to get things just so before you pray. You don't need to clean up your act. You don't need to straighten your tie. You don't need to think things through. Your Father already knows you and everything about you, including exactly where you are and what you need.

Richard Foster wrote:

There are any number of "somethings" preventing us [from praying]. But for now there is one "something" that needs immediate attention. It is the notion— almost universal among us modern high achievers—that we have to have everything "just right" in order to pray. That is, before we can really pray, our lives need some fine-tuning, or we need to know more about how to pray, or we need to study the philosophical questions surrounding prayer, or we need to have a better grasp of the great traditions of prayer. And on it goes. It isn't that these are wrong concerns or that there is never a time to deal with them. But we are starting from the wrong end of things—putting the cart before the horse. Our problem is that we assume prayer is something to master the way we master algebra or auto mechanics. That puts us in the "on-top" position, where we are competent and in control. But when praying, we come "underneath," where we calmly and deliberately surrender control and become incompetent. "To pray," writes Emilie Griffin, "means to be willing to be naïve." [4]

Brother Lawrence, the seventeenth-century author of the spiritual classic *The Practice of the Presence of God*, wrote:

> *For many years I was bothered by the thought that I was a failure at prayer. Then one day I realized I would always be a failure at prayer; and I've gotten along much better ever since.*[5]

And that is not just true of him but of all of us. Jean-Nicholas Grou, the eighteenth-century author of the famous *How to Pray*, wrote:

> *There is no Christian who is not in the same case as the disciples. Every Christian ought to say as humbly as they: "Lord, teach us to pray." Ah! If we were only convinced of our ignorance and of our need of a Teacher like Jesus Christ!*[6]

The first step in prayer is admitting you are taking first steps. Be willing to be naïve. Don't worry about getting it right. Your Father knows what you need before you even ask Him, so relax.

LET GO OF THE NEED TO INFORM OR IMPRESS GOD

If "your Father knows what you need before you ask him," He certainly knows who you really are. You are not going to impress Him with your eloquence, education, or righteousness.

Jesus told the memorable story of the tax collector and the Pharisee. Tax collectors, of course, were among the most despised people in that place and time, and Pharisees were among the most highly respected among the common people because of their meticulous devotion to the law of God. But Jesus cast the characters in His story against type:

> *"Two men went to the Temple to pray. One was a*
> *Pharisee, and the other was a despised tax collector.*
> *The Pharisee stood by himself and prayed this prayer:*
> *'I thank you, God, that I am not a sinner like everyone*
> *else. For I don't cheat, I don't sin, and I don't commit*
> *adultery. I'm certainly not like that tax collector! I fast*
> *twice a week, and I give you a tenth of my income.'*
>
> *"But the tax collector stood at a distance and dared*
> *not even lift his eyes to heaven as he prayed. Instead,*
> *he beat his chest in sorrow, saying, 'O God, be merciful*
> *to me, for I am a sinner.' I tell you, this sinner, not the*
> *Pharisee, returned home justified before God. For those*
> *who exalt themselves will be humbled, and those who*
> *humble themselves will be exalted."*[7]

The Pharisee prayed, basically, "God, I thank You that I'm so great!" He listed the sins he didn't commit (like cheating and adultery) while clearly remaining oblivious to those he did commit (pride and self-righteousness, for example). He apparently thought it was necessary to inform God of the facts and impress God with his virtues ("I fast twice a week, and I give You a tenth of my income"). On the other hand, the tax collector in Jesus' story uttered just one word for every five the Pharisee spoke (in the Greek, at least). He simply admitted his need and asked God for mercy.

Your Father knows what you need before you ask, so you don't need to inform Him or impress Him. You don't have to fill in any blanks for Him, and you don't have to use fancy words or a special tone. He knows you. He knows your faults. He knows your need. So pray simply.

LET GO OF THE NEED TO BEG

You may remember the showdown on Mount Carmel between the prophet Elijah and the prophets of Baal. Elijah challenged them to a duel:

> *"Let the Baal prophets bring up two oxen; let them pick one, butcher it, and lay it out on an altar on firewood—but don't ignite it. I'll take the other ox, cut it up, and lay it on the wood. But neither will I light the fire. Then you pray to your gods and I'll pray to GOD. The god who answers with fire will prove to be, in fact, God."*[8]

So the prophets of Baal went first. They erected an altar, made their sacrifice, and began to pray:

> *They prayed all morning long, "O Baal, answer us!" But nothing happened—not so much as a whisper of breeze. Desperate, they jumped and stomped on the altar they had made.*
>
> *By noon, Elijah had started making fun of them, taunting, "Call a little louder—he is a god, after all. Maybe he's off meditating somewhere or other, or maybe he's gotten involved in a project, or maybe he's on vacation. You don't suppose he's overslept, do you, and*

needs to be waked up?" They prayed louder and louder,
cutting themselves with swords and knives—a ritual
common to them—until they were covered with blood.
This went on until well past noon. They used every
religious trick and strategy they knew to make something
happen on the altar, but nothing happened—not so
much as a whisper, not a flicker of response.[9]

This scene may have been part of what Jesus had in mind
when He said, "When you pray, do not keep on babbling
like pagans, for they think they will be heard because of their
many words."[10] It is like the prayers of some people today who
employ various techniques or tactics intended to get God's
attention, break down His resistance, or even twist His arm
into answering prayer.

But Jesus said your Father knows what you need before
you even ask. Histrionics aren't necessary. Simple, believing
prayer is all it takes, as Elijah's actions and words on Mount
Carmel illustrate:

Elijah told the people, "Enough of that—it's my turn.
Gather around." And they gathered. He then put the
altar back together for by now it was in ruins. Elijah took
twelve stones, one for each of the tribes of Jacob, the same
Jacob to whom GOD had said, "From now on your name
is Israel." He built the stones into the altar in honor of
GOD. Then Elijah dug a fairly wide trench around the
altar. He laid firewood on the altar, cut up the ox, put
it on the wood, and said, "Fill four buckets with water
and drench both the ox and the firewood." Then he said,

"Do it again," and they did it. Then he said, "Do it a third time," and they did it a third time. The altar was drenched and the trench was filled with water.

When it was time for the sacrifice to be offered, Elijah the prophet came up and prayed, "O GOD, God of Abraham, Isaac, and Israel, make it known right now that you are God in Israel, that I am your servant, and that I'm doing what I'm doing under your orders. Answer me, GOD; O answer me and reveal to this people that you are GOD, the true God, and that you are giving these people another chance at repentance."

Immediately the fire of GOD fell and burned up the offering, the wood, the stones, the dirt, and even the water in the trench.

All the people saw it happen and fell on their faces in awed worship, exclaiming, "GOD is the true God! GOD is the true God!" [11]

Elijah's prayer was bold but simple. He didn't beg or cajole. He didn't shout or sermonize. He made a straightforward request, based on his faith in God and the guidance God had already given him. And God answered. Just like that.

This is not to say there is anything wrong with passion, even desperation, in prayer. But passion and desperation are different from begging and wheedling. Desperation, of course, flows from a deep need or strong desire. Passion flows from a heart of faith, a sincere faith based on God's willingness and readiness to answer prayer and give good things to His children. Begging, on the other hand, overflows from a heart that isn't sure God will—or even wants to—answer prayer.

But your Father already knows what you need before you even ask, so you don't need to resort to histrionics or theatrics. Like Elijah, you can ask boldly but simply. Fervently, even, but straightforwardly.

SIMPLY PRAY SIMPLY

I have five wonderful grandchildren. Each, of course, is wonderful in his or her own way. And the middle grandchild (she has two older cousins and two younger siblings) is Calleigh. Not long ago, I had been away on a business trip for a week or so, and when I returned, four-year-old Calleigh excitedly showed me a letter she had written to me while I was gone. It was a single page filled with colorful scribbles and swirls. One or two of the shapes looked like a sun or a flower, and parts of it resembled handwriting. But of course, there was not a single word on it because Calleigh had not yet learned to spell or write.

So I asked her to read it to me. She said, "Dear God, I love God. No, wait. I'll start again. Dear Crappaw, I love Crappaw. Thank you for giving me a good day. I love Crappaw. Dear Calleigh."

I saved the letter and soon recorded her exact words in my journal. I treasure both.

Jesus depicted prayer as something like a child approaching a loving parent (or grandparent). Our words may be primitive. Our prayers may be simple, even painfully so. But God treasures every one. As Richard Foster wrote, "In the same way that a child cannot draw a bad picture so a child of God cannot offer a bad prayer."[12]

And just as Calleigh's letter could hardly have been

simpler—or better—our simplest prayers are the best prayers we can offer, especially when they include four of the simplest, easiest, most basic things we can bring to them.

1. Show up. Author and philosophy professor Peter Kreeft wrote in his book *Prayer for Beginners*:

> *The holy Curé of Ars once noticed an old peasant praying alone in church every day before the Eucharist. The Curé asked the peasant what he did when he prayed, and his answer was the most perfect description of contemplative prayer: "I look at him, and he looks at me.". . . That is all. By a simple act of the will, turn your attention to him.*[13]

Film director and actor Woody Allen is often quoted as saying, "Eighty percent of success is showing up." That is certainly true of prayer. Simply turn your attention to God; that is the beginning of prayer, and it is often the great majority of it as well.

2. Trust. The soul that prays, trusts. The soul that trusts, prays. Wherever you are, remind yourself that God is there. Believe that He is listening. Remember that He is good and loving and that He knows what you need before you even begin to pray. "The best prayer," Julian of Norwich said, "is to rest in the goodness of God, knowing that that goodness can reach down to our lowest depths of need."[14]

3. Listen. "It makes no sense for us to do most of the talking," Kreeft says. "We ought to be listening most of the time."[15] It may take time and practice before you can differentiate between the voice of God and the voices in your head, but it is well worth it to try. This is why silence and solitude are so conducive to prayer; they help us develop listening skills. You may want to repeat the prayer of Samuel: "Speak, your servant is listening."[16] You may find it easier to listen while walking in the woods or sitting alone in a country chapel. You may meditate on the words of author Robert Benson: "I need to listen, listen for the prayer of God that is rising in my heart, perhaps for the prayer that I should be praying rather than the one I am praying."[17]

4. Ask. Remember, "your Father knows what you need before you ask him."[18] So ask. Simply. Do as Richard Foster suggests:

> *In Simple Prayer we bring ourselves before God just as we are, warts and all. Like children before a loving father, we open our hearts and make our requests. We do not try to sort things out, the good from the bad. We simply and unpretentiously share our concerns and make our petitions. We tell God, for example, how frustrated we are with the co-worker at the office or the neighbor down the street. We ask for food, favorable weather, and good health.*[19]

Show up. Trust. Listen. Ask. "On all occasions with all kinds of prayers and requests,"[20] the Bible says. "In every situation, by prayer and petition, with thanksgiving, present your requests to God."[21] "Be direct. Ask for what you need."[22] Just ask. And keep on asking.

> *Lord, teach me to simply pray.*
> *Teach me to pray simply.*

Give me the desire to pray.

And when I do, remind me that my Father already knows what I need, so I can pray as simply and straightforwardly as a child asking for a snack from a loving father.

4

PRAY COMMUNALLY

~

Alone, alone, all, all alone,
Alone on a wide wide sea!
And never a saint took pity on
My soul in agony.[1]

Those lines, from the classic and famous Samuel Coleridge poem "The Rime of the Ancient Mariner," reflect the way many people feel today.

We live in a lonely time.

We are more connected today than ever before—via e-mail, text, social media, and so on. We are often surrounded by people—in stores, at the office, in church. Most of us know far more people than our grandparents and great-grandparents ever did. Yet feelings of disconnectedness and aloneness are epidemic.

There may be other people around. There may be plenty of people in your life. But who has time for relationships anymore? We work long hours trying to meet unrealistic expectations. We race from one commitment to another. We struggle to keep our kids active and the lawn mowed and the laundry done. New neighbors moved in two years ago and we still haven't introduced ourselves.

Thirty years ago, when researchers asked a cross-section of Americans how many close confidants they had—people with whom they could discuss their innermost thoughts, fears, or joys—the most common response was three. When they asked again ten years ago, the most common answer—from one in four respondents—was zero. Zilch. Nada. None. If the survey were to be taken today, it seems likely the news would be even worse.

Ironically enough, if you feel alone, you're not alone!

A WORLD IN A WORD

When Jesus' earliest disciples asked Him to reveal His prayer secrets to them, He shared a way to pray that resembled the kind of prayer they had practiced all their lives but revolutionized it. He demonstrated something that Christians have since called the Lord's Prayer or the Our Father. And from its very first sound, its first syllable, He gave a single word that contains and encloses a whole world: *our*.

He said the following:

"Pray like this:

'Our Father in heaven!
    May your Name be kept holy.
May your Kingdom come,
    your will be done on earth as in heaven.

Give us the food we need today.
Forgive us what we have done wrong,
    as we too have forgiven those who have wronged us.
And do not lead us into hard testing,
    but keep us safe from the Evil One.
For kingship, power and glory are yours forever.
Amen.'"[2]

Notice that Jesus said to pray, "*Our* Father. . ." Not "My. . ." but "Our. . ." It is a small word—just three letters long in English, but there is a whole world in that single little word, *our*. Because it means you and I never pray alone.

WE PRAY WITH JESUS

When Jesus prayed, He addressed His prayers to the One He called Father. When He shared His prayer secrets with His followers, He included them—and us—with Him in that partnership. He told them—and us—to pray not to Jesus' Father only but to pray, "*Our* Father." He incorporated us with Him in that tiny word *our*. In other words, when you pray, "*Our* Father," you pray with Jesus.

This is at least a part of what He meant when He told His followers to pray in His name:

"Whatever you ask in my name, this I will do, that the Father may be glorified in the Son." [3]

"If you ask me anything in my name, I will do it." [4]

"Truly, truly, I say to you, whatever you ask of the Father in my name, he will give it to you. Until now you have asked nothing in my name. Ask, and you will receive, that your joy may be full." [5]

A mysterious and powerful symbiosis occurs whenever a follower of Jesus prays. The person praying is approaching the throne of God as a follower of Jesus—His representative, who has authority to ask things on behalf of the Son of God

Himself (more on this in chapter 7). But even as that is happening, Jesus is acting as the Advocate of all "who come to God through him. He lives forever to intercede with God on their behalf." [6]

Andrew Murray, in his classic work on prayer, *With Christ in the School of Prayer*, wrote:

> *We participate, not only in the benefits of [Jesus'] work, but in the work itself. This is because we are His Body. The Head and the members are one: "The head cannot say to the feet, I have no need of thee" (1 Corinthians 12:21). We share with Jesus everything He is and has. "The glory which Thou gavest me, I have given them" (John 17:22). We are partakers of His life, His righteousness, and His work. We share His intercession, too. He cannot do it without us.*
>
> *"Christ is our life"; "No longer I, but Christ liveth in me." The life in Him and in us is identical; it is one and the same. His life in Heaven is a life of continuous prayer. When it descends and takes possession of us, it does not lose its character. It becomes a life of continuous prayer in us, too. It is a life that without ceasing asks and receives from God.*
>
> *This is not as if there were two separate currents of prayer rising upwards—one from Him and one from His people. A substantial life-union is also a prayer-union. What He prays passes through us, and what we pray passes through Him. He is the angel with the golden censer. "Unto Him there was given much incense"—the secret of acceptable prayer—"that He*

should offer it with the prayers of all the saints upon the golden altar" (Revelation 8:3). We live and abide in Him, the Interceding One.[7]

You never pray alone. Whenever you pray, you pray with Jesus, and Jesus prays with and for and in and through you.

WE PRAY WITH THE SPIRIT

Anyone who prays much at all will know that there are times when cohesive thought—let alone prayer—seems impossible:

When I don't know the circumstances. I am frequently asked to pray for a person or a situation without knowing the details. It may be an obviously desperate but unspoken request from someone in a prayer meeting. Or a cryptic note on social media: "Please keep Butch in your prayers." Or a painfully terse text message: "Pray!" At such times I can't pray, "Lord, heal," or "Send protection," or anything similarly specific.

When I am overwhelmed with emotion. When my third grandchild was diagnosed with cystic fibrosis, I cried with my daughter and her husband after they told me and my wife the news. When we got home, I held my wife in my arms and cried with her. Before going to bed, I went to the prayer chair in my study and cried with God. I may not have formed any words that evening other than, "Oh, God," and "Oh, Lord."

When I'm not sure what God's will is. Over the years I have frequently been asked to pray for a vast variety of situations or outcomes: for someone to get a specific job, for someone's house to sell, for someone to get out of jail, for someone to close a business deal. Often, even after I'd spent time listening to God and asking for His guidance, His will and His purpose remained unclear to me.

At such times it helps me tremendously to remember that I never pray alone. The Bible says:

> *The Spirit helps us in our weakness. For we do not know what to pray for as we ought, but the Spirit himself intercedes for us with groanings too deep for words. And he who searches hearts knows what is the mind of the Spirit, because the Spirit intercedes for the saints according to the will of God.*[8]

Whenever I pray, I pray with the Holy Spirit. Sometimes I will verbally rely on this verse in my prayer, saying something like, "Holy Spirit, I don't know what to pray here, so I rely on Your intercession to fill in the blanks. Help me in my weakness. Intercede for me with groans I can't understand. Form the thoughts and speak the words I can't begin to express."

Whenever you pray—even when you don't know what to say or ask—you don't pray alone; you pray with the Spirit. He intercedes for you according to the will of God, the Bible says, and He does so even when you *do* know what to say. He is always praying with you, sometimes focusing your thoughts and polishing your words, and at other times making sense when all you have are tears or grunts or stammers.

WE PRAY WITH THE CHURCH

When Jesus told his followers to pray, "*Our* Father," he gave them a communal prayer. I think he did this for several reasons.

He intends for us to pray together. Jesus' words reveal an assumption that His followers would frequently gather to pray. He said:

> *"Truly, I say to you, whatever you bind on earth shall be bound in heaven, and whatever you loose on earth shall be loosed in heaven. Again I say to you, if two of you agree on earth about anything they ask, it will be done for them by my Father in heaven. For where two or three are gathered in my name, there am I among them."* [9]

Sometimes we pray in a large group, such as a public worship service. We may pray in a smaller group, in a home, or in a prayer meeting. Or we may pray with a prayer partner.

Just as I discovered long ago that losing weight is much easier when my wife participates with me, I have found it helpful to enlist prayer partners, whether close or distant. My first prayer partner helped me through a period of struggle in my prayer life by promising to show up on my doorstep every weekday morning at 7:30 a.m. for prayer—and also by promising *not* to call if he couldn't make it. On the days he didn't appear by 7:35 or so, I prayed alone, since I was already awake and sipping my first cup of coffee anyway! That way he helped me stay faithful in prayer when he was present *and* when he was absent.

He intends for us to pray in unity. The passionate intercession of Jesus in John 17 (often called His "high priestly prayer") includes repeated prayers for unity among His followers. He said:

> *"Holy Father, keep them in your name, which you have*

given me, that they may be one, even as we are one. . . .
I do not ask for these only, but also for those who will
believe in me through their word, that they may all be
one, just as you, Father, are in me, and I in you, that
they also may be in us, so that the world may believe
that you have sent me. The glory that you have given me
I have given to them, that they may be one even as we
are one, I in them and you in me, that they may become
perfectly one, so that the world may know that you sent
me and loved them even as you loved me." [10]

Clearly, Jesus intends for His followers to be united. No
wonder He taught us to say, "*Our* Father." If we are truly
followers of Jesus, we will share His desire for unity among
His followers. If we are truly followers of Jesus, we will pray
for unity between ourselves and other Christians. If we are
truly followers of Jesus, we will reflect His priorities and
remember them as we pray. We will pray for our brothers
and sisters around the world. . .and down the street. We will
seek opportunities to join with others in prayer. We will pray
in the awareness that, as Peter Tze Ming Ng of the Chinese
University of Hong Kong says, "The real church is—and always
has been—multicultural. . . . When we think of the church
we must conjure up a picture not of people like ourselves,
but of people of all colors and shapes and ages, women and
men speaking different tongues, following different customs,
practicing different habits, but all worshiping the same Lord." [11]

"God is found in union and agreement," said the French
theologian Pasquier Quesnel. "Nothing is more efficacious
than this in prayer." [12]

He intends for us to pray in harmony. When you pray, *"Our Father,"* you are praying in harmony with people of other lands and languages. Whether in Gaelic:

Ar n-Athair a tha air nèamh: gu naomhaichear d'ainm.
Thigeadh do rìoghachd.
Dèanar do thoil air an talamh,
mar a nìthear air nèamh.
Tabhair dhuinn an-diugh ar n-aran làitheil,
agus maith dhuinn ar fiachan,
amhail a mhaitheas sinne dar luchd-fiach.
Agus na leig ann am buaireadh sinn,
ach saor sinn o olc.
[Oir is leatsa an Rìoghachd, agus an Cumhachd
agus a' Ghlòir, gu sìorraidh.]

Or Japanese (transliteration):

Ten ni imasu watashitachi no chichi yo
Mina ga agameraremasu yō ni
O-kuni ga kimasu yō ni
Mikokoro ga ten de okonawareru yō ni
chi de mo okonawaremasu yō ni
Watashitachi no higoto no kate o
kyō mo o-atae kudasai
Watashitachi no oime o o-yurushi kudasai
Watashitachi mo, watashitachi ni
oime no aru hitotachi o yurushimashita
Watashitachi o kokoromi ni awasenaide,
aku kara o-sukui kudasai

Kuni to chikara to sakae wa, tokoshie ni
anata no mono dakara desu

Or Swahili:

Baba yetu uliye mbinguni,
Jina lako litukuzwe,
Ufalme wako uje,
Mapenzi yako yatimizwe,
hapa duniani kama huko mbinguni.
Utupe leo riziki yetu.
Utusamehe deni zetu,
kama sisi nasi tuwasamehevyo wadeni wetu.
Na usitutie majaribuni,
lakini utuokoe na yule mwovu.
[Kwa kuwa ufalme ni wako, na nguvu, na utukufu,
hata milele.]

When you pray, "*Our* Father," your prayers harmonize with the prayers of followers of Jesus around the world. In fact, many Christians practice—or are discovering—the daily office, a set of prayers at specific times that allow them to harmonize their prayers with others around the world and throughout history. Dr. Scot McKnight has written a helpful book, *Praying with the Church*, that will help anyone enter into these ancient rhythms of prayer. In fact, in that book he also mentions another way in which we pray with the Church:

We confess the communion of saints. This means we
believe there is a spiritual unity among all Christians,

all over the globe and all through history: Christians who are praying in heaven now and on earth below, saints who have gone before us and who will follow us. Sometimes we narrow our scope in this confession to those who are now alive with us, but the Church has always believed that we are ever surrounded by a "great cloud of witnesses" (as the author of the letter to the Hebrews puts it).[13]

Andrew Murray pointed out the beauty, privilege, and power of praying with the Church in *With Christ in the School of Prayer*:

What an extraordinary privilege united prayer is! What a potential power it has! Who can say what blessing might be gained:

if the believing husband and wife knew they were joined together in the Name of Jesus to experience His presence and power in united prayer (1 Peter 3);

if friends were aware of the mighty help two or three praying in concert could give each other;

if in every prayer meeting the coming together in the Name, the faith in His presence, and the expectation of the answer stood in the foreground;

. if in every church united, effective prayer were regarded as one of the chief purposes for which they are banded together;

if in the universal Church the coming of the Kingdom and of the King Himself were really a matter of unceasing, united crying to God![14]

Whenever you pray—whether by yourself or with others, whether spontaneously or otherwise—you don't pray alone; you pray with the Church.

WE PRAY WITH ALL CREATION

When Paul wrote those lyrical words about the Spirit of God interceding "for us with groanings too deep for words,"[15] he also said:

> *For all creation is waiting eagerly for that future day when God will reveal who his children really are. Against its will, all creation was subjected to God's curse. But with eager hope, the creation looks forward to the day when it will join God's children in glorious freedom from death and decay. For we know that all creation has been groaning as in the pains of childbirth right up to the present time. And we believers also groan, even though we have the Holy Spirit within us as a foretaste of future glory, for we long for our bodies to be released from sin and suffering. We, too, wait with eager hope for the day when God will give us our full rights as his adopted children, including the new bodies he has promised us.[16]*

Theologian N. T. Wright comments on this passage:

> *In one of his greatest pieces of writing and of theology (Romans 8.18–27), [Paul] explains prayer in terms of the Spirit groaning within the Church as the Church groans within the world. The call to pray this clause*

of the prayer is therefore the call to be Annunciation-people; Gethsemane-people; and, yes, Calvary-people. We are called to live and pray at the place where the world is in pain, so that the hopes and fears, the joy and pain of the whole world may become, by the Spirit and in our own experience, the hope and fear, the joy and pain of God.[17]

When we pray, "*Our* Father," we are praying with the whole world, with all of God's groaning creation. And this communal praying not only blesses others; it enlarges us. Theologian and pastor James Mulholland wrote:

When I begin to pray for those beyond my doorstep, then I begin to pray for heaven on earth. I am reminded that God, like any good father, doesn't play favorites. I can quit maneuvering for better position on his lap. I can stop acting as if God's love for others will diminish his love for me. I can relish my relationship with God without ignoring my responsibility to my brothers and sisters. . . . When I am reminded to pray for their needs, I am transformed. I often discover my needs are not as serious as I thought. When I pray for the woman dying of cancer, my cold doesn't seem such a burden. When I pray for those dying of starvation in Sudan, my desire for a new house seems selfish. Praying for the needs of others always helps me see how my blessings exceed my needs.[18]

If you are a follower of Jesus Christ, you never pray alone. You pray with Jesus. You pray with the Holy Spirit. You pray with the church in heaven and on earth, around the world and throughout history. And you pray with all creation.

Even as I pray now, Lord Jesus, I ask for Your assistance.
Holy Spirit, pray with me in my weakness.
Father, hear my prayer.
Thank You for the realization that I never pray alone.
Let my prayers come before You now, in unity with all my brothers and sisters in heaven and on earth, around the world, and throughout history, to make us all one and to heal the hopes and fears, the joy and pain of the whole world.
In Jesus' name, amen.

5

Pray Relationally

~

My son, Aaron, was in the third or fourth grade when his teacher suggested to the class that they invite their parents to give short talks about their jobs for career day.

At that time, I had written and published four or five books and had been a full-time writer for a year or two. I worked from home. My home office was a four-by-six-foot corner of our master bedroom—a chair and a tall shelf unit with a drop-leaf desk. Aaron was accustomed to seeing me in that chair, on my primitive laptop computer, for hours at a time.

When the teacher made her way around the room and got to Aaron, she asked, "Aaron, what does your father do for a living?"

Aaron shrugged. "Nothing," he said. "He just plays on the computer all day."

If pressed, I imagine Aaron could have given a little more insight into his father's livelihood. After all, he knew about the books I had produced—he had even read one or two. But while some people attached a certain glamour or mystique to being an author, there was never anything impressive or sensational about it—or about me—to Aaron. He saw me every day. We tossed baseballs to each other. We wrestled on the floor. We crawled in and out of the same hollow tree (though he fit inside much more easily). We sang "The Simpsons Sing the Blues" in the car together. He didn't attach labels such as "professional writer" or "author" or "speaker" to me. I was just Dad.

Believe it or not, that is the sort of attitude Jesus urges on His followers. It is fundamental to the red-letter prayer life. Because prayer—as Jesus taught it—can be and should be relational.

WORD ONE

The first word Jesus says on the subject of prayer is the word *Father.* Literally.

In both Greek and Aramaic, the word that begins the prayer we commonly call the Lord's Prayer is *Father.* Jesus was not the first person in history (even in Judaism) to address God as Father, but He clearly surprised His contemporaries not only with the relationship He claimed with His Father but also with the relationship He urged His followers to claim.[1]

Those early followers of Jesus, who first heard and recorded the words of the Lord's Prayer, used many terms and titles in praying to God. Here is a short list of the way they probably addressed God in prayer:

> *Lord our God and God of our Fathers*
> *The God of Abraham, Isaac, and Jacob*
> *The Great, Mighty, and Revered God*
> *The Most High God*
> *The Creator of All*
> *King, Helper, Savior, and Shield*
> *The Shield of Abraham*
> *The Reviver of the Dead*
> *Master of Mighty Deeds*

The God who is Holy
Redeemer of Israel
Adonai our God
The King who loves righteousness and justice
The Builder of Jerusalem
Lord God, King of the universe
Living and eternal King [2]

Such ways of addressing God are perfectly proper, but when Jesus chose a mode of address for His example of how to pray, He took a far more *personal* approach. With one word, Jesus redefined prayer as relational more than ritual. He taught His followers that a close, intimate relationship *with* God is the basis of prayer *to* God. He said, "When you pray, say: 'Father. . .'" [3]

"Abba."

"Papa."

"Daddy."

It is impossible to overemphasize how important this is to the red-letter prayer life. It may be the most important thing Jesus taught about prayer. In that single word He conveyed a number of deep and impactful truths.

WHEN WE SAY, "FATHER," WE ASSUME A RELATIONSHIP

"It is in the personal relation to the living God, and the personal conscious fellowship of love with Himself, that prayer begins," wrote Andrew Murray. "It is in the knowledge of God's Fatherliness, revealed by the Holy Spirit, that the power of prayer will be found to root and grow." [4]

The use of the word *Father* in prayer assumes a relationship. As missionary and evangelist E. Stanley Jones wrote, "The first thing in prayer is to get God. If you get Him, everything else follows. Allow God to get at you, to invade you, to take possession of you."[5]

In her book *Two-Way Prayer*, Priscilla Brandt described an encounter with a friend named Ann at a retreat. Ann's parents had managed a Christian retreat center. Ann and her minister husband were involved in an exciting church, and Priscilla—or Perky, as friends call her—was leading Ann and other pastors' wives in a prayer retreat. Priscilla told the group to close their eyes and imagine a place of beauty, quiet, and tranquility. She continued:

> "Imagine someone in the distance coming toward you. As he gets closer, notice that it is Jesus." A tear slid down Ann's cheek. I continued. Another tear, then another. I noticed her face becoming blotchy and her nose turning red. I knew she was muffling her sobs. The others sat quietly and peacefully. Ann opened her eyes and reached into her purse for a handkerchief. Then she left the room.
>
> After the session I asked, "Ann, what happened?"
>
> "You told us to visualize a quiet place," she said. "I did. I imagined myself sitting on a hill at my parents' retreat center. Not far away was a natural cave with a large stone alongside. It depicts Christ's tomb and I loved going there as a child. We used it for Easter sunrise services.
>
> "Then you said, 'Now, look up and see Jesus coming to you.' Perky, I waited for him to come out of the

tomb. Something inside me told me he had to come out of the tomb—but he didn't come. He didn't come. I waited. No Jesus!" She was holding the damp crumpled handkerchief to her runny nose.

I leaned close and lowered my voice. "Ann, does Jesus seem real to you?"

She shook her head no.

"Does he seem alive in your life?" Again, no.

"Do you want him to be your Friend. . .alive and real?"

She nodded yes.

"Have you ever asked him to be your Friend?"

Her eyes widened, her mouth dropped open. "No, I guess I never really did ask him! Perky, thank you! I've got to go now. I want to go home. I know just what I have to do!"[6]

The red-letter prayer life begins there, with a relationship with God through faith in and surrender to Jesus, the Son of God. It happens when a human soul sincerely says, "Lord, have mercy on me, a sinner. Take me as I am. I give You my sins, myself, my life. With Your grace and constant help, I will follow You and serve You as my Savior, Friend, Teacher, and Lord, moment by moment, day by day, for the rest of my life."

Then, writes theologian N. T. Wright, "as soon as one becomes a Christian, he or she can and must say, 'Our Father'; that is one of the marks of grace, one of the first signs of faith."[7] No wonder Jesus made *Father* the first word in the prayer He modeled for His followers. With that word, He said, in effect, "Pray relationally."

WHEN WE SAY, "FATHER," WE AVAIL OURSELVES OF INTIMACY

No one would have argued if Jesus had begun His model prayer differently. He could have said, "When you pray, say, 'Master. . .' " Or "When you pray, say, 'Lord. . .'" Or "When you pray, say, 'King. . .' " None of those would have been inappropriate then, and none are inappropriate now.

But Jesus struck a much more intimate tone in teaching His followers to pray. He encouraged a prayer posture that is less like a subject approaching a king and more like a child climbing into a father's lap. And those early disciples clearly took His praying and teaching to heart, as shown in Paul's later writings:

> *You have not received a spirit that makes you fearful slaves. Instead, you received God's Spirit when he adopted you as his own children. Now we call him, "Abba, Father."*[8]

> *Because we are his children, God has sent the Spirit of his Son into our hearts, prompting us to call out, "Abba, Father."*[9]

My daughter, Aubrey, is a beautiful, intelligent, and accomplished woman. She is a married woman and a mother of three children. She refers to me as her father, of course. But there are times—precious times—when she, grown woman that she is, still calls me Daddy (and not always when she wants a favor). It never fails to warm my heart and, yes, make me even more willing than ever to make her dreams come true.

According to Jesus, you can claim that kind of intimacy with God. You can tell Him things and rely on such familial closeness. You can ask Him things on the basis of that relationship. In fact, Bible teacher and author Larry Crabb suggests that such intimacy is actually the key, the source, the fountainhead of all true and effective prayer. He writes:

Relational prayer is the center of all true prayer. . . .
Fix relational prayer in the exact center of your life. See
every day as an opportunity to relate more intimately
with your heavenly Papa and to bring His kingdom
into your specific circumstances by the way you relate to
others. That's what Jesus did, in the power of the Spirit.
And He invites us to do the same thing.

As that happens, as Christians across the world put
relational prayer in the center of their lives, the church
will recover its power. Union with God will become a
growing reality. Desire for Him will surpass every other
desire. We'll suffer well, we'll be good stewards of blessings,
and we'll live to reveal what our Papa is like to a watching
world, to our spouses, kids, friends, and colleagues.[10]

To quote Andrew Murray again:

Do not be thinking of how little you have to bring to
God, but of how much He wants to give you. Just place
yourself before, and look up into, His face; think of His
love, His wonderful, tender, pitying love. . . . Is it not
wonderful? to be able to go alone with God, the infinite
God. And then to look up and say: My Father! [11]

WHEN WE SAY, "FATHER," WE ACCEPT AN APPRENTICESHIP

When I was growing up in a near suburb of Cincinnati, Ohio, my father owned and operated a Mr. Softee ice cream truck. Six days a week (from April to October, I think) he left the house early in the morning and returned late at night after driving through the streets and neighborhoods of Florence and Erlanger, Kentucky, selling ice cream (vanilla and chocolate), snow cones (or "ice balls," as most kids in the area called them), and various other high-calorie concoctions to people who heard the bell that announced his arrival.

Sometimes during the summer, once school was out, I would go with him on a Saturday. While a dad who owns an ice cream franchise may seem like a dream come true to some people, there wasn't a whole lot to do in a motorized ice cream parlor. . .except eat. How I avoided obesity (until much later in life) is a mystery to this day. Eventually, however, I was old enough to sit on the stool in the back of the truck while my father drove and wait on customers when he stopped—if only for the relief from boredom it offered. My compensation for ten or twelve hours of labor on those summer Saturdays (other than eating all the ice cream I liked) was one whole dollar. (If the United States Department of Labor ever heard of this outrage, they never acted.)

For obvious reasons, perhaps, from the ages of twelve to about thirty, ice cream held little appeal to me—which may be part of the reason I never once considered following in my father's footsteps and becoming a Mr. Softee ice cream man.

In Jesus' day, however, there wouldn't have been any question about it. Sons and daughters did whatever their parents did. If your father was a stonecutter, you became his apprentice and then his partner, until one day you took over the business. And then *your* son became *your* apprentice. And so it went.

So when Jesus told His followers to relate to God as a father, He said it in that context. And very likely, they understood it in that context. And though our cultural context today is quite different, the content of Jesus telling us to pray relationally still applies. In other words, when you and I say, "Father," we should understand that we are not only assuming a relationship and availing ourselves of intimacy; we are also accepting an apprenticeship.

N. T. Wright applies this understanding to one of Jesus' most heartfelt prayers, just before His arrest, trial, and execution:

Calling God 'Father' was not simply comfortable or reassuring. It contained the ultimate personal challenge.

That is why, in the Garden of Gethsemane, he called God 'Father' once more. In John's gospel Jesus uses the image of father and son to explain what he himself was doing. In that culture, the son is apprenticed to the father. He learns his trade by watching what the father is doing. When he runs into a problem, he checks back to see how his father tackles it. That's what Jesus is doing in Gethsemane, when everything suddenly goes dark on him. Father, is this the way? Is this really the right path? Do I really have to drink this cup? . . . What we see in Gethsemane is the apprentice son, checking back one more time to see how the Father is doing it. . . . And the learning process was only complete when he said,

'Father, into your hands I commend my spirit.' . . .
That's why calling God 'Father' is the great act of
faith, of holy boldness, of risk. Saying 'our Father' isn't just
the boldness, the sheer cheek, of walking into the presence
of the living and almighty God and saying, 'Hi, Dad.'
It is the boldness, the sheer total risk, of saying quietly,
'Please may I, too, be considered an apprentice son.'[12]

The red-letter prayer life is relational. It is intimate. And it is an acceptance of apprenticeship to the Father that will have us, like Jesus, learning by watching the Father at work, checking in frequently to see what the Father is doing, and getting better and better at it as we say, over and over, "Father," "Abba," "Papa," "Daddy."

Father, thank You that I can call You Father.
Abba, teach me to pray relationally, to allow You to
get at me, to invade me, to take possession of me, now
and always.
Papa, I place myself before You. I look up into Your
face and see Your wonderful, tender, pitying love. I look
up and say: my Father!
Daddy, give me not only the great act of faith, of
holy boldness, of risk, of walking into the presence of
the living and almighty God and saying, "Hi, Dad,"
but also the boldness, the sheer total risk, of saying
quietly, "Please may I, too, be considered an apprentice,
watching You, learning from You, doing what I see You
doing, and getting better and better at it, moment by
moment and day by day?"
In Jesus' name, amen.

6

Pray Confidently

—

In October 2012, my wife, Robin, and I traveled to Germany to conduct a retreat for about five hundred youth pastors and children's pastors in Dillenburg, about 100 kilometers (63 miles) north of Frankfurt. Though I had come down with a virus on the flight to Germany, our visit was proceeding well, the response at the conference was gratifying, and we looked forward to an extra day of relaxing and sightseeing before flying home to Ohio.

As the retreat wound down, we learned that a superstorm named Sandy was expected to strike the east coast of the United States at about the time our return flights were scheduled to land and take off through JFK airport in New York City. Forecasters were predicting cataclysmic effects from the storm, which was predicated to merge with *another* storm front and make landfall not far from the New York area. Area governors were preemptively declaring a state of emergency, and airlines started announcing flight cancellations. It looked like we would be stranded at JFK—perhaps for days—assuming we even managed to take off from Frankfurt.

I sent a short text message to a family member who works for the airline on which we had booked our flights, asking for advice. Should I try to contact the airline in Germany or the United States? Should I try to delay our departure or cancel our plans and fly back early? Should I try to reroute our flights? Within an hour or two, I received a response to my text message, informing me that our return flights had been changed. Instead of flying through New York, we were rebooked on a flight from Frankfurt to Cincinnati through Detroit.

The storm's high winds and heavy flooding devastated areas of New York and New Jersey. Thousands of homes were destroyed, thousands of flights were canceled, and millions of people were left without electricity—some of them for weeks. At least 159 people died as a direct or indirect result of the storm.

My wife and I arrived in Detroit while Sandy still raged. We didn't completely escape the storm's effects, however. As Sandy moved inland, it transformed from a hurricane to a blizzard. Our flight from Detroit to Cincinnati was canceled, but the same family member who had rebooked our flights had reserved a rental car for us while we were in the air, out of touch, unaware. The 250-mile drive from Detroit to our home just north of Cincinnati took more than eight hours, twice as long as it would have under normal conditions, but we were grateful to be home and safe.

It sure helps to have the right connections.

A Friend in High Places

"It's not *what* you know," says the old cynical adage, "it's *who* you know." The idea of that saying is that you can be the smartest person around, but if you don't have the right connections—a friend or two in high places—you won't get far. You won't get that raise, that promotion, that title, that recognition, that plum position on intelligence or ability alone; it takes the right connections, too. In fact, in some organizations or situations, you don't even need ability; you just have to be related to the boss, or at least be on his or her good side.

When the first and closest followers of Jesus asked Him to school them in prayer, Jesus started with the words, "Our Father in heaven."[1] As the first two words in the Lord's Prayer call us to pray communally and relationally, so the third and fourth words—*in heaven*—also instruct us in the red-letter prayer life. They offer hope. They offer assurance. They offer confidence of acceptance and consideration.

When Jesus said to pray, "Our Father in heaven," He wasn't just throwing words around. He didn't add the "in heaven" part as just a nice little flourish. The entire prayer He modeled to His disciples, which we call today the Lord's Prayer or the Our Father, contained barely sixty words (as it was recorded in Matthew's Gospel), and every word is important. Every word fairly drips with truth and rings with value. Those two tiny words—*in heaven*—should make a huge difference in how we pray—and how much we pray.

They are easily misunderstood, however. To say, "Our Father in heaven," is not to locate God in time and space, much less to define Him, to say what He is like. Rather than saying what (or where) God is, that short phrase distinguishes Him, differentiates Him from what He is not.

PRAY CONFIDENTLY BECAUSE YOUR FATHER IN HEAVEN IS NOT YOUR EARTHLY FATHER

As a pastor, I have met countless people who struggle to relate to God and experience His love because their concept of a father has been formed—or rather, malformed—by an unfulfilling or unhealthy relationship with their earthly father. Others never knew their father, so trying to relate to God as a father is like someone who has been blind from birth trying to understand the color green.

That is why the red-letter prayer life, the life of prayer as defined by Jesus, is so important. Because when Jesus tells us to pray, "Our Father in heaven," He distinguishes our heavenly Father from all earthly fathers. He says, in effect, that to pray like Jesus prayed is to understand the following things.

Your Father in heaven is not absent. He is not an absentee dad. When Moses encountered the burning bush in the wilderness of Midian, God spoke to him from the bush, saying:

> *"I have surely seen the affliction of my people who are in Egypt and have heard their cry because of their taskmasters. I know their sufferings, and I have come down to deliver them out of the hand of the Egyptians and to bring them up out of that land to a good and broad land, a land flowing with milk and honey."* [2]

God said, "I have *seen*. I have *heard*. I *know*. I have *come*." God saw and heard and knew everything His people were going through; He was never absent, never unconcerned, never disconnected from them. And the same is true of you. Your Father in heaven sees, hears, knows, and cares about every detail of your life. And He comes to you. He is with you. "He will not leave you or forsake you." [3]

Your Father in heaven is not neglectful. Singer and songwriter Harry Chapin scored a number one hit with the song "Cat's in the Cradle." The lyrics tell the story of a man who welcomes a son into the world. "But there were planes to catch and bills to pay," the song says, painting a picture of a growing boy who repeatedly longs for his dad to spend time with him and play with him. But the father is too busy and answers, "Not today."

Chapin's song is a tearjerker and more so because many people can identify with that experience of fatherly neglect. But it is not a picture of your Father in heaven. He is an attentive Father. According to the psalmist David, "He observes everyone on earth; his eyes examine them,"[4] and "The eyes of the LORD watch over those who do right; his ears are open to their cries for help."[5] And Peter said, succinctly, "He cares for you."[6] He never sleeps.[7] He is never distracted. He never loses sight of you and is never too busy for you.[8]

Your Father in heaven is not capricious. One of William Shakespeare's most famous plays, *King Lear*, depicts an aging king who decides to divide his realm among his three daughters according to the love they express for him. When his youngest—and most virtuous—daughter, Cordelia, refuses to take part in the charade, the king banishes her and entrusts himself and his kingdom to his remaining daughters, who are manipulative and disloyal. Everyone in the story pays dearly for the king's impulsive and unpredictable behavior. It is a sad and all-too-familiar depiction of the harm that can be done by a capricious father, whether caused by addiction, mental illness, or something else.

But Jesus differentiates your "Father in heaven" from any earthly father. When He tells us to pray to "our Father in heaven," He points toward the One described by the psalmist:

But you, O LORD, are enthroned forever;
you are remembered throughout all generations. . . .

Of old you laid the foundation of the earth,
and the heavens are the work of your hands.
They will perish, but you will remain;
they will all wear out like a garment.
You will change them like a robe, and they will pass away,
but you are the same, and your years have no end.
The children of your servants shall dwell secure;
their offspring shall be established before you.[9]

Your Father in heaven says, "Though the mountains be shaken and the hills be removed, yet my unfailing love for you will not be shaken."[10]

Your Father in heaven is not abusive. If you have suffered abuse of any kind—verbal, emotional, mental, physical, sexual—from an earthly father or stepfather, please hear Jesus' call to pray to "our Father in heaven" as a clear, ringing distinction from that kind of father and that kind of treatment. Your heavenly Father is so far removed from that behavior that the difference cannot be measured. David describes your Father in heaven:

The LORD is merciful and gracious,
slow to anger and abounding in steadfast love.
He will not always chide,
nor will he keep his anger forever.
He does not deal with us according to our sins,
nor repay us according to our iniquities.

For as high as the heavens are above the earth,
so great is his steadfast love toward those who fear him;
as far as the east is from the west,
so far does he remove our transgressions from us.
As a father shows compassion to his children,
so the LORD shows compassion to those who fear him.[11]

Regardless of whatever faults or shortcomings your earthly father had—and all fathers have at least some—you can pray confidently because your Father in heaven is not your earthly father.

PRAY CONFIDENTLY BECAUSE YOUR FATHER IN HEAVEN IS NOT DISTANT

It would be easy to misunderstand the phrase "our Father in heaven"—and many have—without understanding what Jesus meant by the word *heaven*. Theologian N. T. Wright explains:

When the Bible speaks of heaven and earth it is not talking about two localities related to each other within the same space-time continuum or about a nonphysical world contrasted with a physical one but about two different kinds of what we call space, two different kinds of what we call matter, and also quite possibly (though this does not necessarily follow from the other two) two different kinds of what we call time. . . . In the Bible heaven and earth are made for each other. They are the twin interlocking spheres of God's single created reality. . . . God's space and ours—heaven and earth, in

other words—are, though very different, not far away
from one another.[12]

Later in the same book, Wright says, "In the Bible heaven and earth are made for each other. They are the twin interlocking spheres of God's single created reality."[13] My mental picture when I heard as a boy, "Our Father, who art in heaven," was of God way up in the sky, far past the clouds, beyond the sun, moon, and stars. . .somewhere. But the image Jesus paints is not a picture of distance but of nearness, not of detachment but of difference. To borrow Wright's terms, our Father in heaven is not constrained by space, matter, or time; He controls those things. He is the Father of whom the psalmist David sang:

> *O LORD, you have examined my heart*
> *and know everything about me.*
> *You know when I sit down or stand up.*
> *You know my thoughts even when I'm far away.*
> *You see me when I travel*
> *and when I rest at home.*
> *You know everything I do.*
> *You know what I am going to say*
> *even before I say it, LORD.*
> *You go before me and follow me.*
> *You place your hand of blessing on my head.*
> *Such knowledge is too wonderful for me,*
> *too great for me to understand!*
> *I can never escape from your Spirit!*
> *I can never get away from your presence!*

If I go up to heaven, you are there;
  if I go down to the grave, you are there.
If I ride the wings of the morning,
  if I dwell by the farthest oceans,
even there your hand will guide me,
  and your strength will support me.[14]

PRAY CONFIDENTLY BECAUSE YOUR FATHER IN HEAVEN IS NOT LIMITED

There are so many things I would do for my two children if I could. My wife and I were always careful to provide for them without spoiling them. We did our best to give them good things while also insisting that they learn to save and plan to earn and buy things themselves. While other families we knew gave their children new cars on their sixteenth birthdays (or soon after), we acquired a used Jeep Cherokee for both of our kids to share once they both had driver's licenses. Even then, we didn't give the car to them; they were expected to make payments to us and traded weeks as the primary driver. Our daughter, however (who is the older of our two children), would tell you that she got the better end of the deal because her younger brother was grounded so often that she got to drive the Jeep far more often than he did.

Still, while I didn't want to raise spoiled kids (and if you knew them today, I'm sure you would agree that they both matured into thoroughly unspoiled, well-rounded adults), there have been many times I wished I could have given them more—or better—things than our financial situation usually permitted. Disney World, for example (they only visited twice as kids). And college (we sent them both to fine schools, but I wish we hadn't had to cut as many corners as we did).

But our Father in heaven is not limited. He is all-knowing, all-seeing, all-powerful. He is not a creature but the Creator. He is no victim of circumstances but the victor over every circumstance. He is not bound by the laws of nature—or by the state of the economy. He transcends every limitation. He owns and controls and rules all. He is your boss's Boss. He is your king's King. He is Ruler of Storms and the Hope of the desolate. When Jesus tells us to pray to "our Father in heaven," He is telling us to pray in that reality, in that awareness, of God's unlimited ability. Pastor and author Bill Hybels wrote:

> *Many of us have pressing personal needs and serious problems that ravage our lives, but we don't ask God for help because somewhere, well beneath our surface layer of faith and trust, we don't believe God has the power to do anything about them.*
>
> *The fact is, of course, that God is capable of handling any problem we could bring him. Creating planets isn't much of a problem for him. Neither is raising the dead. Nothing is too difficult for God to handle—but he's waiting for us to recognize his power and ask for his help.*[15]

Your Father in heaven is able. He is able to anoint and depose kings. He is able to part waters. He is able to raise the dead. He is able to do what He says He will do.[16] And He "is able to bless you abundantly, so that in all things at all times, having all that you need, you will abound in every good work."[17] "For no word from God will ever fail."[18] "With God all things are possible."[19] Nothing is too hard for Him.[20]

PRAY CONFIDENTLY BECAUSE YOUR FATHER IN HEAVEN IS NOT RELUCTANT

Our Father in heaven loves to answer prayer. He is an all-willing, all-giving, generous, and resourceful Father to us. He is not only *"able* to bless you abundantly,"[21] but He is also utterly willing and even anxious to do so. To quote Hybels again:

> *God is interested in your prayers because he is interested in you. Whatever matters to you is a priority for his attention. Nothing in the universe matters as much to him as what is going on in your life this day. You don't have to pester him to get his attention. You don't have to spend hours on your knees or flail yourself or go without food to show him you really mean business. He's your Father; he wants to hear what you have to say. In fact, he's waiting for you to call.*
>
> *If one of my kids ever called me and said, "Dad, please, please, please, I beg you, I petition you, I plead with you to listen to my humble request," I'd say, "Time out. I don't like the underlying assumption here. You don't have to go through all those gymnastics. What in my life is more important than you? What gives me greater pleasure than meeting your needs? What can I do for you?"*
>
> *"Come into my presence," says God. "Talk to me. Share all your concerns. I'm keenly interested in you,*

because I'm your Father. I'm able to help, because all
power in heaven and earth is mine. And I'm listening
closely, hoping I will hear your voice."[22]

When Jesus says to pray, "Our Father in heaven," He is
not suggesting we should pray to overcome God's reluctance
but to ignite our Father's willingness. As E. M. Bounds wrote:

Earthly parents, though evil in nature, give for the
asking, and answer to the crying of their children. The
encouragement to prayer is transferred from our earthly
father to our Heavenly Father, from the evil to the good,
to the supremely good; from the weak to the omnipotent,
our Heavenly Father, centering in Himself all the
highest conceptions of Fatherhood, abler, readier, and
much more than the best, and much more than
the ablest earthly father. "How much more," who can
tell? Much more than our earthly father, will He supply
our needs, give us all good things, and enable us to meet
every difficult duty.[23]

The Father to whom you pray is not your earthly father
but is the supremely good, gracious, always present, always
involved, all-knowing, all-seeing, all-powerful, all-willing,
generous, and resourceful Father in heaven. So pray. Pray confidently. Pray to your Father in heaven.

Our Father in heaven,
my soul glorifies you,[24]

and my spirit rejoices in God my Savior,
my Father in heaven,
for you see me in my humble state, and
you are attentive to me right where I am.
You are able to bless me abundantly, so that in all things
at all times,
having all that I need, I will abound in every good
work.
You are the Mighty One who has already done great
things for me—
the Holy One, whose mercy extends to all who fear you,
from generation to generation.
You have performed mighty deeds with your arm;
you have scattered the proud and deposed rulers from
their thrones,
but you have lifted up the humble.
You have filled the hungry with good things
and sent the rich away empty.
You have helped me,
always present, always close, all-powerful, and all-willing.
Father in heaven, increase my faith,
and embolden my prayers,
in Jesus' name, amen.

7

PRAY COOPERATIVELY

〜

He's an ant. An ant with issues.

"I always tell myself there's got to be something better out there," he says, "but maybe I think too much. I think everything must go back to the fact that I had a very anxious childhood. My mother never had time for me. You know, when you're the middle child in a family of five million, you don't get any attention."

He goes on, rising from the therapist's couch. "I was not cut out to be a worker. . . . I feel physically inadequate. My whole life, I've never been able to lift more than ten times my own body weight. And when you get down to it, handling dirt is—ew, not my idea of a rewarding career. . . . The whole system makes me feel. . .insignificant."

Of course, those are among the first lines in the opening scenes of the animated DreamWorks film *Antz*. But they also reflect the way many people think. . .or come to feel. Insignificant. Inadequate. Overlooked.

You've felt it, haven't you? Maybe you're even feeling it now.

There is within each of us a longing to be useful. A desire to be needed—to contribute to the lives of others in a meaningful way, to know we've made a difference somehow. It is a hunger to be a part of something important, something worthwhile, something great.

And yet so often we feel exactly the opposite. You may not be the middle child in a family of fifty million, like the lead character "Z" in *Antz,* but you may still long to fit in somewhere, to believe that you're important, that you have something to offer, that somewhere there is a place, a role, a function where you can fit in and do something valuable and fulfilling.

I believe the red-letter prayer life is key to the fulfillment of those desires.

THREE PETITIONS

Those of us who are familiar with the Lord's Prayer tend to forget that until His first followers came to Him and asked Him to share His prayer secrets with them, there was no such thing as the Lord's Prayer. Elementary, I know. But it is important to remember that simple fact and let it inform our prayer lives.

For example, if you had been present when Jesus uttered those first few words, "Our Father in heaven," what would you have expected to come next? Forget that you know (if you do) the phrases that follow those words in the Lord's Prayer. What would you have predicted as Jesus' next words in teaching His disciples how to pray?

Judging from the way many of us have witnessed and learned prayer, we might have expected Him to say, "Our Father in heaven. . .most glorious, most wonderful, most high God, who inhabits the praises of His people, we honor and glorify You today." Am I right? That sounds familiar and appropriate.

Or we might have anticipated something along these lines: "Our Father in heaven. . .we come before You right now in gratitude for all Your blessings and loving-kindness toward us, for creating, preserving, sustaining, and guiding us in this life and to the life that is to come—for the gifts of life, family, friends, sound minds, and clear consciences." Right? Again, that might have fit the occasion.

On the other hand, hearing those first few words, we might have assumed something like, "Our Father in heaven, we come before you broken and contrite, confessing our sins and begging Your forgiveness, for we cannot ascend Your holy hill with filthy hands and unclean hearts."

But of course, we know that Jesus chose none of those directions. Maybe on another day, He would have. Maybe if different people had asked for His advice on prayer, He would have suggested something else. But He didn't. He followed "Our Father in heaven" with three simple but striking petitions. He said:

> *"Pray like this:*
> *'Our Father in heaven!*
> *May your Name be kept holy.*
> *May your Kingdom come,*
> *your will be done on earth as in heaven. . . .'"* [1]

Succinct, no? But so profound and substantial. You may recall the words from the King James Version of the Bible: "Hallowed be thy name. Thy kingdom come. Thy will be done in earth, as it is in heaven."[2] That single word *Thy* (or *Your* in today's English) in all three phrases is so important. Andrew Murray wrote:

While we ordinarily first bring our own needs to God in prayer, and then think of what belongs to God and His interests, the Master reverses the order. First, Thy name, Thy kingdom, Thy will; then, give us, forgive us, lead us, deliver us. The lesson is of more importance than we think. In true worship the Father must be first, must be all. The sooner I learn to forget myself in the desire that He may be glorified, the richer will the blessing be that prayer will bring to myself. No one ever loses by what he sacrifices for the Father.[3]

This is how Jesus says to pray: cooperatively. That is, prayer—according to Jesus—is quite different from how we picture it and approach it. We tend to think of prayer in terms of getting answers. We want to learn to get good *at it* so we can get good *from it*. This is natural and understandable, of course; we are only human. But there is nothing natural and understandable about the red-letter prayer life; it is supernatural and mysterious.

According to Jesus, prayer is first and foremost about the Father, not about us. It is not about getting things from God but entering into partnership with God. It results in blessings, not as a result of seeking blessings but from seeking the Blesser—His glory, His kingdom, His will.

Take Time to Be Holy, a one-year devotional drawn from the writings of Samuel Logan Brengle, puts it this way:

A young man felt called to mission work in China, but his mother offered strong opposition to his going. An agent of the mission, knowing the need of the work

*and vexed with the mother, one day laid the case before
Hudson Taylor.*

*"Mr. Taylor gently suggested our praying about it,"
he said. "Such a prayer I have never heard before! It
seemed to me more like a conversation with a trusted
friend whose advice he was seeking. He talked the
matter over from every point of view—the side of the
young man, of China's needs, of the mother and her
natural feelings, and also my side. It was a revelation
to me. I saw that prayer did not mean merely asking
for things—much less asking for things to be carried
out by God according to our ideas—but that it means
communion, fellowship, partnership with our heavenly
Father."[4]*

Jesus says prayer is a cooperative venture, a partnership between
you and God, in which you align with *His* mind before you
speak *your* mind. It is a demanding and thrilling process by
which you think and say and do the following three things.

1. Pray, "I Guard Your Reputation"

"Hallowed be thy name," the King James Version of the
Bible phrases the first request. It is a phrase that is as important
to understand as it is easy to misunderstand, not least because
various Bible translations and versions express it differently:

"Uphold the holiness of your name" (Common English
Bible).
"Let your name be kept holy" (God's Word Translation).
"May your name be honored" (J. B. Phillips translation).

"May your name always be kept holy" (New Century Version).

It is possible that Jesus, in including this phrase in the prayer He taught His followers, was echoing the *Kedushat HaShem*, an ancient prayer that has been passed down through the centuries as the third blessing of the *Amidah*, the daily blessings recited by observant Jews. Early in their evening prayers, Jews will say:

> *You are holy, and your Name is holy, and your holy ones praise you every day. Blessed are you, Adonai, the God who is holy.*[5]

If so, however, Jesus rendered the affirmation of the *Kedushat HaShem* as a petition. He changes "You are holy, and your Name is holy," to "May your Name be kept holy." According to Philip Keller:

> *What we would say in modern idiom is something like this: "May You be honored, revered, and respected because of who You are. May Your reputation, name, person, and character be untarnished, uncontaminated, unsullied. May nothing be done to debase or defame Your record."*[6]

Implicit in the request—if it is sincere—is a commitment on the part of the person praying to guard God's reputation and protect the integrity and holiness of "HaShem," the Name. It is a request and an attitude like that of a friend of mine, who would send her children to school every morning with the admonition, "Remember who you are," repeating the family name and making it clear that they were expected to bring honor, not shame, to that name.

The 1992 movie *A League of Their Own* features Tom Hanks in the role of the drinking and carousing team manager Jimmy Dugan. When he takes over the team, he makes it clear that he is uninterested in anything other than fulfilling his contract and cashing his paycheck. He sleeps through games. He berates his own players. But then the team starts to win, and he starts to care. Finally, when they make the playoffs, he decides to lead the team in a locker-room prayer.

"Lord," he begins, "hallowed be Thy name." He then proceeds to ask for swift feet and mighty bats before thanking God for "that waitress in South Bend" with whom he had enjoyed a one-night stand and concluding his prayer with a plea for his team to finish the season well. The scene shows that Jimmy Dugan had some knowledge of the Lord's Prayer—after all, he quoted, "Hallowed be Thy name." But the words were clearly meaningless to him, because profane actions cannot help to "hallow" God's name.

What does it mean to "hallow" God's name? It means at least three things:

1. Trusting God. Once, when God's people were wandering in the Sinai wilderness after their deliverance from slavery in Egypt, they complained because of a lack of water. So God told Moses to speak to the face of a cliff where they had camped, promising that water would flow from the rock. Rather than speaking to the rock, however, Moses struck it with his staff— which had played a part in several miracles back in Egypt.

And the LORD said to Moses and Aaron, "Because you did not believe in me, to uphold me as holy in the eyes of the people of Israel, therefore you shall not bring this assembly into the land that I have given them."[7]

"Because you did not believe in me," God said, "to uphold me as holy in the eyes of the people." Believing God, trusting Him, and taking Him at His word "hallows" His name and upholds His reputation.

2. Obeying God. When God gave His commandments to His people, He told them, "So you shall keep my commandments and do them: I am the LORD. And you shall not profane my holy name, that I may be sanctified among the people of Israel."[8] In other words, a lifestyle of submission and obedience to God "hallows" His name—not a legalistic Puritanism but a winsome, day-by-day pursuit of God and His ways.

3. Rejoicing. When David's second attempt to return the ark of the covenant—the symbol of God's presence with His people—to Jerusalem was successful, he was so overcome with joy that he threw off his kingly robes and danced with abandon in the holy procession. His wife, Michal, however, was watching from a window (notice that she wasn't even in the procession!). She berated her husband because, she said, "he exposed himself like a fool in the sight of the servant women of his officials!" But David answered:

"I was dancing to honor the LORD, who chose me instead of your father and his family to make me the leader of his people Israel. And I will go on dancing to

honor the LORD, *and will disgrace myself even more. You may think I am nothing, but those women will think highly of me!*"[9]

Joy—in worship, in trial, in the details of daily life—honors God. When your life exudes "the joy of the LORD,"[10] God's name is hallowed.

The red-letter prayer life is not a "Jimmy Dugan" prayer life. It does not say, "Hallowed be Thy name," while cussing and carousing. It will not say, "May Your reputation, name, person, and character be untarnished, uncontaminated, unsullied," while living a selfish, profane life. It cannot say, "May nothing be done to debase or defame Your record," while acting in unholy ways. It is not only a prayer but also a life of trusting God, obeying Him, and "always rejoicing."[11]

2. PRAY, "I ENLIST IN YOUR CAUSE"

The second petition in the prayer Jesus taught His followers is "May Your kingdom come." He spent much of His time and effort during His three years or so of active ministry defining and explaining God's kingdom. He said it is like a priceless treasure.[12] He said it can be hidden,[13] yet it can grow in beauty and influence like you wouldn't believe.[14] He said it is living and growing within His followers.[15] He showed that it is a mysterious, wonderful, healing, life-giving thing.

Frederick Buechner wrote:

> *It is not a place, of course, but a condition. Kingship might be a better word. . . . As a poet, Jesus is maybe*

*at his best in describing the feeling you get when you
glimpse the Thing itself—the kingship of the king
official at last and all the world his coronation. It's like
finding a million dollars in a field, he says, or a jewel
worth a king's ransom. It's like finding something you
hated to lose and thought you'd never find again—an
old keepsake, a stray sheep, a missing child. When the
Kingdom really comes, it's as if the thing you lost and
thought you'd never find again is yourself.*[16]

The kingdom of God is the "crazy and utterly risky vocation" of Jesus, N. T. Wright says. "And when he taught his disciples to pray, Thy Kingdom Come, he wanted them to pray that he would succeed in it."[17]

But He wants us to do more than that. To pray, "May Your kingdom come," is to say, "I enlist in Your cause. I adopt Your agenda. 'Here am I; send me.' "[18] As Philip Keller points out:

*If I sincerely, earnestly, and genuinely implore God to
come into my life and experiences, there to establish
His Kingdom, I can only expect that there is bound to
be a most tremendous confrontation. It is inevitable
that there will follow a formidable conflict between His
divine sovereignty and my self-willed ego.*

*When I pray, "Thy kingdom come," I am willing to
relinquish the rule of my own life, to give up governing
my own affairs, to abstain from making my own
decisions in order to allow God, by His indwelling
Spirit, to decide for me what I shall do. . . .*

When Christ uttered the simple yet profound

petition, "Thy kingdom come," He envisaged His own future kingdom on earth and also the very Spirit of the living God coming into a human heart at regeneration to make it His holy habitation. He pictured the King of kings so permeating and invading a life that His authority would be established in that person's mind and will. He saw a human being as a temple, an abode, a residence of the Most High. But He knew that only when such an occupied heart is held and controlled by the indwelling Spirit could it be truly said that here indeed is a part of the spiritual Kingdom of God where His will was done on earth.

Of course, such a relationship conveys with it enormous benefits and privileges. It is no small thing to be a member of this select, spiritual community. It is a most lofty and noble honor to be counted among the citizens of God's heavenly Kingdom.[19]

Praying, "May Your kingdom come," is a visual exercise for me. As I say those words, every day (and usually multiple times a day), I survey in my mind's eye a panorama of where I want God's kingdom to spread. The picture starts in me, with my heart and life, and flows outward, like a river. I "see" God's kingdom transforming my family, my children and their workplaces, my grandchildren and their schools, my neighborhood and church. I envision God's kingdom changing "the east side" of my community, where people live in poverty and fear, enslaved by drugs and alcohol. I visualize God's kingdom invading the nearby prison I pass often in my travels until it becomes a place of reclamation and renewal.

I see my nation's capital, revolutionized by wisdom and teamwork and unity. I picture the Middle East (it's amazing how far and fast you can travel in prayer) and see Jerusalem, a city I've come to love, where residents and neighbors alike enjoy peace and prosperity.

When I pray, "May Your kingdom come," I pray for mercy, grace, and peace—in me and in those around me. When I pray, "May Your kingdom come," I pray for His kingdom to invade seeking souls and hungry hearts. I pray for love to conquer all. I pray for wars to end. I pray for the Church to be healthy, united, and effective. I pray for justice. I pray for diseases to be eradicated. I pray for racial reconciliation, sensible government, a healthy environment, and a vigorous economy.

Presidential candidate John Kerry famously accepted his party's nomination for the presidency of the United States of America by appearing onstage at the 2004 Democratic National Convention in Boston, Massachusetts, saluting, and saying, "I'm John Kerry and I'm reporting for duty." Regardless of political persuasion, that is what a follower of Jesus Christ does when he or she prays, "May Your kingdom come." It means, "I enlist in Your cause. I adopt Your agenda. I am reporting for duty."

3. Pray, "I Do What You Say"

The third petition in the prayer Jesus taught His disciples is "May Your will be done, on earth as it is in heaven." As Andrew Murray wrote, "Because the will of God is the glory of heaven, the doing of it is the blessedness of heaven. As the will is done, the kingdom of heaven comes into the heart.

And wherever faith has accepted the Father's love, obedience accepts the Father's will."[20]

We tend to attach that last phrase—"on earth as it is in heaven"—only to the third petition ("May your will be done"). But it is quite possible—linguistically and theologically—that Jesus intended that phrase to modify all three petitions that precede it. In other words, He taught us to pray, "May Your name be kept holy on earth as it is in heaven, may Your kingdom come on earth as it is in heaven, and may Your will be done on earth as it is in heaven." After all, God's name is hallowed perfectly and thoroughly by every inhabitant of heaven: "Holy, holy, holy," they cry, "throwing down their golden crowns beside the crystal sea."[21] And his kingdom is undisputed and untrammeled in heaven, where the Lamb who was slain receives all the "power and wealth and wisdom and strength and honor and glory and praise"[22] that are His due. And of course, the host of heaven does God's will instantly, constantly, completely, and worshipfully.

Of course, implicit in the prayer for God's will to be done "on earth as it is in heaven" is the praying soul's own submission to God's will. It makes no sense to pray for God's will to be done everywhere but in me. Thus, "May Your will be done, on earth as it is in heaven" means "I will do what You say."

The words of the Lord's Prayer were proven and polished in the Lord's passion, of course. On the night He was betrayed, Jesus prayed in the garden of Gethsemane, anticipating His approaching arrest, trial, and crucifixion, "My Father, if it is possible, may this cup be taken from me. Yet not as I will, but as you will."[23] He prayed twice more, asking for an escape hatch, but saying, "May your will be done."[24]

Jesus not only taught, "May Your will be done, on earth as it is in heaven." He prayed it. He lived it "to death—even death on a cross!"[25]

Praying, "May Your will be done, on earth as it is in heaven," is an act of surrender, willingness, and eager, obedient intention. It is an attitude like that reflected in the daily habit of Bishop Taylor Smith, a British army chaplain, who wrote:

> *As soon as I awake each morning I rise from bed at once. I dress promptly. I wash myself, shave and comb my hair. Then fully attired, wide-awake and properly groomed, I go quietly to my study. There, before God Almighty and Christ my King, I humbly present myself as a loyal subject to my Sovereign, ready and eager to be of service to Him for the day.*[26]

That is the red-letter prayer life. It is cooperative prayer, prayer that partners with God in guarding His reputation, advancing His cause, and doing His will. It is prayer that, realistically speaking, may lead to a Gethsemane or a Calvary. But it will also lead you to the throne, to "Mount Zion, to the city of the living God, the heavenly Jerusalem."[27]

> *God, my Father in heaven,*
>   *You are holy, and Your name is holy.*
>   *"May You be honored, revered, and respected because of who You are.*
>   *May your reputation, name, person, and character be untarnished, uncontaminated, unsullied.*

May nothing be done to debase or defame Your record" [28]*—least of all, anything I might think, or say, or do.*

May Your kingdom come.

May it rule my heart and life, and may it flow from me like rivers of living water.[29]

May your kingdom prevail in and around all those I love and emanate throughout my home, family, workplace, neighborhood, country, and world.

And may Your will be done in me, on this day and every day that is to come.

May your will be done always and everywhere, until the whole earth is filled with the knowledge of Your glory, as constantly and comprehensively as the waters cover the sea.[30]

In Jesus' name, amen.

8

PRAY PRACTICALLY

—

Not long ago, my friend and fellow author, Michelle Medlock Adams, had an experience involving her daughter, Abby. She posted this on Facebook:

I just have to take a minute and share a testimony. Abby is on her way to visit her boyfriend in Lexington, and she just called crying, saying she had just missed being in a terrible accident. A car pulled out of the median, almost side-swiping her, causing Abby to swerve into the right lane and three cars ended up off the road because of one driver's poor timing, poor judgment, or whatever. But here's what I wanted to share. . .

Abby is driving my car today, which is bigger and better on the highway, because her VW bug needs a window replaced. (It broke last night.) As we drove Abby's car over to get fixed this morning, the Lord prompted me to pray protection over Abby. I didn't hear a big, loud voice from the sky—just that inner prompting, that still small voice. I usually pray over both of my girls, every morning, but in the craziness of this morning (trying to get Abby out the door to Lexington and hit a deadline by 9 a.m.), I hadn't prayed my normal prayer or had my devotions yet. God is so faithful. He gently nudged me to pray and so I did—praying that Abby's guardian angels would surround her car as she traveled to and from Lexington this weekend. And I prayed over Ally and her car, too, since she is a new driver in LA and that LA traffic is a little overwhelming at times. It only took me a minute to say those quick prayers, but I am so thankful I followed the Holy Spirit's prompting.[1]

Some people might say that the prompting Michelle felt and the subsequent accident her daughter escaped was a coincidence. Others might even suggest that God is too busy to be concerned with one young woman's safety on the expressway; after all, He has bigger fish to fry, so to speak, with wars and famines and epidemics happening around the world.

But Jesus would disagree.

FROM THE SUBLIME TO THE MUNDANE

When Jesus taught His first followers to pray, He gave them a framework of fewer than five dozen words. He started, "Our Father in heaven," and then proceeded to three requests that draw the person praying into the mission and priorities of Jesus Himself: "May Your name be kept holy, may Your kingdom come, and may Your will be done on earth as it is in heaven." Or put another way, "Glorify Your name, spread Your kingdom, accomplish Your will."

Those petitions may not be what we would naturally say as we begin praying. They may not even be what we would have expected Jesus to say, if we had been there when He first spoke these words. But they make perfect sense.

His next words, however—the fourth petition in the Lord's Prayer, as it is commonly called—take a somewhat surprising turn. From the sublime to the mundane, you might say. From heavenly to earthly. From extraordinary to ordinary. He says we should pray, "Give us today our daily bread."[2]

Really, Jesus? Bread? After instructing us to pray about the holiness of God's name, the coming of His reign, and the accomplishment of His sovereign will. . ."give us today our daily bread"?

"Yes," He would say. In a word, "Bread."

There is a slight difference in the wording between Matthew's and Luke's account of this request. Matthew, who includes the Lord's Prayer as part of the Sermon on the Mount discourse—which was very likely intended to be the *mishnah*, or condensed teachings, of Rabbi Jesus—records this request as "Give us today our daily bread."[3] In Luke, Jesus gives His disciples this prayer in response to their request to "teach us to pray"[4] and records this petition as "Give us each day our daily bread."[5] It is generally thought to be a distinction without a difference, as the point is basically the same in both cases.

In any case, those few words from the prayer Jesus taught His disciples make it clear that praying for the most basic, practical, ordinary needs of daily life is perfectly consistent with praying also for such high and lofty things as God's reputation, kingdom, and will. In other words, when you pray, Jesus says, pray practically.

PRAY FOR YOUR EVERY NEED

Chances are, since you're reading these words, you are pretty far removed from the world of those who first heard the Lord's Prayer and its request, "Give us this day our daily bread." You have access to books! You probably have bread in your cupboard, maybe even some meat and vegetables in your freezer. A little change in your pocket, a few pairs of shoes in your closet, a car in your garage. Your standard of living is probably so far removed from those who first received Jesus' instructions on prayer as to be nearly immeasurable.

When Jesus said to pray, "Give us this day our daily bread," He was urging on His followers a day-by-day dependence on God for the most basic, elemental human needs. It wasn't figurative. It wasn't symbolic of "what we're going to need today," as we generally understand it when we pray. It was literally a prayer for bread. And literally a prayer for today.

I think it still is.

I think we pray best when we exhibit a day-by-day dependence on God for the most basic, elemental human needs. Oh, sure, you can pull a frozen pizza from the freezer for dinner tonight, but has God not provided that? Long before Jesus taught His followers the Lord's Prayer, God spoke these words to His people through Moses:

> *When you have eaten and are satisfied, praise the LORD your God for the good land he has given you. Be careful that you do not forget the LORD your God, failing to observe his commands, his laws and his decrees that I am giving you this day. Otherwise, when you eat and are satisfied, when you build fine houses and settle down, and when your herds and flocks grow large and your silver and gold increase and all you have is multiplied, then your heart will become proud and you will forget the LORD your God. . . . You may say to yourself, "My power and the strength of my hands*

have produced this wealth for me." But remember the
LORD your God, for it is he who gives you the ability to
produce wealth. [6]

Some people say grace both before *and* after meals because it
is one thing to give thanks when you're hungry—and another
thing to give thanks when you are full. Similarly, it is one thing
to pray, "Give us this day our daily bread" when you don't
know where your next meal is coming from—and another
thing to pray it just as sincerely when your cupboard is full.

Jesus didn't say to pray, "Give us this day our daily bread,"
when we are in need. He said, "When you pray, say. . .Give us
this day our daily bread." It is a prayer for all seasons because
we should never say to ourselves, "My power and the strength
of my hands have produced this wealth for me."[7] We should
daily remember the Lord our God who gives us the ability to
produce wealth, to buy bread, and even to chew it, swallow it,
and digest it.

"Give us this day our daily bread" does go beyond bread,
however. For years now, I have maintained a daily prayer blog [8]
on which I post a (usually) short prayer every morning. Some
of the prayers are quite personal, such as the prayer I posted
when my granddaughter was diagnosed with cystic fibrosis.
But I also post prayers of praise or thanks. Some of the prayers
are in response to current events. Others are ancient prayers or
famous prayers. One of my favorite types of prayers, however,
are what I call text prayers, which I type into the text app on
my phone and send to God—a screen grab of which I then
post on the blog. Many of those text prayers echo the prayer
Jesus gave His disciples. Here are a few examples:

Give us this day our daily breath.
Give us this day our daily break.
Give us this day our daily coffee.
Give us this day our daily discovery.
Give us this day our daily strength.
Give us this day our daily fun.
Give us this day our daily work.
Give us this day our daily health.
Give us this day our daily oxygen.
Give us this day our daily creativity.
Give us this day our daily hope.

You get the idea. Each prayer is a reminder that, just as the children of Israel had to depend on God for a daily delivery of manna to their doorstep, so praying, "Give us this day our daily bread," teaches me to pray for the things I need—even those things I could take for granted. Maybe *especially* those things I could take for granted.

"Give us this day our daily bread" also teaches me to pray and trust God to meet my needs, not to give me everything I want. "Daily bread" is not a giant-screen television. "Daily bread" is not a hefty Christmas bonus. "Daily bread" is not a new car, bigger house, or season tickets. The words of James challenge me:

> *The reason you don't have is that you don't pray! Or you pray and don't receive, because you pray with the wrong motive, that of wanting to indulge your own desires.*[9]

Jesus teaches us to "seek first the kingdom of God,"[10] and His reputation and His will, and *then* to pray practically—not for God to indulge our selfish desires but to meet our every need, from the most mundane to the most miraculous.

PRAY DAILY

A prayer for daily bread is a daily prayer. Pastor and author Richard Andersen wrote:

> *The word Jesus uses here for "daily" is unique. It is not found anywhere in classical or New Testament Greek. Some people thought Matthew made up the word— that is, until 1947, when they unearthed the Dead Sea Scrolls. Among all the shards of pottery and scraps of papyrus and parchment was a shopping list—and Jesus' word was on the list. It was the designation of a category: the items a housewife needed to purchase every day in the agora, the marketplace. A recently-found, fifth-century Egyptian papyrus also uses the term on a list of expenses to identify "a daily ration."*
>
> *The emphasis [is] on the daily reception of that which cannot be stored up for the future.*[11]

When Jesus said to pray, "Give us this day our daily bread," He clearly intended (assumed, even) for it to be a daily prayer. Of course He did. He was speaking—initially, at least—to people for whom prayer defined the rhythms of their lives. They didn't go to work or take breaks or make appointments according to the hands of a clock; they did so according to the times of prayer that set the rhythms of their daily lives. We live in a different world than Jesus' first followers, of course. Prayer no longer defines and dictates our schedules. . .which may be part of the reason we live in a different world.

My wife, Robin, and I once took ballroom dancing lessons. On one occasion, when we were attempting to waltz for the first time, our instructor watched us for a moment and then said, in a pleased tone, "You're doing well."

And we were, if I do say so myself. She had started by counting the beat (one-two-three, one-two-three) but then had stopped as we one-two-threed around the floor.

"You've found the rhythm, haven't you?" she asked.

"Oh yeah," I said. "The rhythm's no problem."

"We're both musicians," Robin offered.

"Ohhh," the instructor said. "I should have known."

When we asked her to explain, she told us that she often had to teach people to dance who had no sense of rhythm, no knowledge of music. In such cases, she had to try to teach them how to hear the rhythm in the music and coordinate their steps with that rhythm, which meant spending a lot of time counting and clapping, trying to get the rhythm of each dance into their heads. . .and feet.

Suddenly, I felt like a star pupil (a new feeling for me), until our instructor looked at my feet and said something like, "I've just never seen a musician dance so poorly."

From the very first, God installed a rhythm into His creation, a daily rhythm, one of "evening and morning."[12] I think the life of Jesus reflected that rhythm. Mark 1:35 says:

Very early in the morning, while it was still dark, Jesus got up, left the house and went off to a solitary place, where he prayed.[13]

Luke reported:

At daybreak, Jesus went out to a solitary place. [14]

These are reported quite matter-of-factly, as though they were nothing unusual. In fact, it is likely that Jesus, as a Jewish man, made time to pray three times a day, as David wrote and sang about:

> *Evening and morning and at noon*
> *I utter my complaint and moan,*
> *and he hears my voice.* [15]

Praying three times a day was a common practice, not only for Jews in the time of David and Daniel[16] and Jesus, but also beyond. The *Didache*, a manual of Christian life from around the turn of the first century, includes the Lord's Prayer followed by the instruction to pray it three times a day. Many Christians around the world still follow that practice today.

I have found that a morning and evening time of prayer and quietness with God is my "minimum daily requirement." For you, it might be three times a day. . .or once. But I firmly believe it won't be less than daily, not if you want to experience the red-letter prayer life.

Anne Lamott wrote:

> *I've heard it said that every day you need half an hour*
> *of quiet time for yourself, or your Self, unless you're*
> *incredibly busy or stressed, in which case you need an*
> *hour. I promise you, it is there. Fight tooth and nail*

to find time, to make it. It is our true wealth, this
moment, this hour, this day.[17]

How different will your world be if it is defined by daily prayer? How different will your days be? Your family? Your work?

How might you change if you "seek first the kingdom of God,"[18] and His reputation and His will, and *then* pray practically—for your every need, from the most mundane to the most miraculous? How might your attitude change if you start seeing your daily bread—or pizza, hamburger, or casserole—as having been kindly and generously provided by your loving Father? How might your life change if you develop a day-by-day dependence on God for your every need and see Him answer—sometimes even with manna from heaven?

Day by day the manna fell;
Oh to learn this lesson well!
Still by constant mercy fed,
Give me, Lord, my daily bread.[19]

PRAY UNSELFISHLY

Jesus taught His followers to pray for daily bread but not for their daily bread alone. He said to pray, "Give *us* this day *our* daily bread." It is an indication that our practical prayers should include others. N. T. Wright wrote:

It is impossible to pray for our daily bread, or for
tomorrow's bread today, without being horribly aware of
the millions who didn't have bread yesterday, don't have

any today, and in human terms are unlikely to have any
tomorrow either. . . . We should be praying this prayer
not just for the hungry, but with the hungry, and all
who are desperate from whatever deep need. [20]

When you pray for your practical needs, pray also for the
needs of others. Pray for the hungry—in your community and
around the world. Pray for the desperate. Pray for all in need.
Pray for the grace to share your bread with others and the
wisdom to do it well. James Mulholland wrote:

I was watching a television program in which a
Christian from Sudan was being interviewed. He asked,
"How can our rich Christian brothers and sisters in
America ignore the fact that we in Sudan are starving
to death?" I thought to myself, "I'm glad I don't have to
answer that question!" And then the Holy Spirit tapped
me on the shoulder and said, "You do."
What would you say to that man? I think I would
have to apologize. I wouldn't want to admit how many
times my prayer has really been "Give me this day
my daily luxuries." I wouldn't want to confess to how
seldom I have even thought about his plight. I wouldn't
want to have to tell him that American Christians give
only about 3 percent of their income to their churches
and charities. I certainly wouldn't want to mention how
much food we throw away after a church dinner.
That man in Sudan and I both pray, "Give us this
day our daily bread." For him, it is a cry of desperation.
For me, it needs to become a vow of generosity. When I

*say those words, I'm not asking for bread for myself. I'm
twenty pounds overweight. I could use a little less daily
bread. When I pray "Give us this day our daily bread,"
I am pledging to do all in my power to see that my
brother in Sudan has daily bread.*

*"Give us this day our daily bread" is a prayer of
equality. It is a recognition of God's interest in more
than just my needs. God cares for the needs of all. . . .
He wants everyone to have enough.[18]*

Pray practically. Pray, "Give us this day our daily bread." Pray
it for yourself. Pray for your needs. Pray it every day. Pray it
unselfishly, for those for whom daily bread is not figurative
but a literal, pressing, desperate need.

> *Lord, I come to You in my need and say, "Give us
> this day our daily bread."*
> *Meet my need, especially _____.*
> *I ask You for the grace to pray every day, "Give us
> this day our daily bread," to hungrily take each morning
> the daily manna of Your presence.*
> *And help me to pray, "Give us this day our daily
> bread," for and with all those who didn't have bread
> yesterday, don't have any today, and are unlikely to have
> any tomorrow.*
> *Move me and others to pray and give and work so
> that everyone can have enough, in Jesus' name, amen.*

9

PRAY SPECIFICALLY

~

Bartimaeus heard the sounds of a crowd approaching from his customary spot on the roadside near Jericho.

He couldn't see them, however. He was blind.

He was a familiar sight to others on their way in and out of Jericho, though there were no familiar sights to him. Nonetheless he knew his post by the number of steps he counted from his hovel nearby and the cool shade of the palm tree under which he would sit while he begged for alms from all who passed. Though his eyes were dark, his hearing and sense of smell were sharp; he could distinguish—with great accuracy—a child from an adult, a man from a woman, a Jew from a Gentile, and even a priest from a tax collector.

So as he heard the crowd approaching that day, he saw nothing but discerned much. He knew that Yeshua, the healer from Galilee, had come to the bustling oasis town near the river Jordan. He heard people excitedly mentioning him as they passed Bartimaeus on the road. So the approach of the crowd—the smell of dust kicked up by many feet and the murmurs of many people talking and traveling in a cluster—told him all he needed to know.

He sat quietly until he judged the group to be just the right distance away. Then he banged his walking stick on the underside of his begging bowl.

"Yeshua! Son of David! Have mercy on me!"

He paused. Listened. The shuffle of the crowd stopped

and nearby voices cursed him and told him to be quiet. He ignored them.

He banged the bowl again. "Son of David! Have mercy on me!"

He lifted his face skyward and listened. He heard several voices, but one spoke with a different quality. "Call him over," it said.

Someone stepped closer to him. He heard several people telling him to get up. A strong hand took him by the arm, and a man spoke: "He's calling you."

He shrugged off his dirty cloak and scrambled to his feet. He let himself be led away from his palm tree, still clutching his stick and bowl. He could tell by the sounds around him—shuffling and muttering—that he was being guided into the center of the crowd.

His guides stopped, so he stopped, too. The crowd fell silent. He waited.

A single voice, then. A man's voice. Unhurried and unhurrying. "What do you want Me to do for you?"

It was the voice of the healer. Yeshua. The man some said was the Messiah, the Sun of Righteousness. Bartimaeus suddenly realized that he stood before Yeshua, his walking stick in one hand and his begging bowl, as always, upturned in the other.

He lowered the hand with the bowl and placed it behind his back. Then he answered. "Rabbi. . .I want to see."

"Go," Yeshua said. "Your faith has healed you."

Immediately the darkness fled. And the first thing he saw was his healer's smiling face.[1]

BEYOND "BLESS ME"

A blind beggar stood before Jesus. And Jesus asked, "What do you want Me to do for you?"

It seems like a strange question. Ludicrous, even. After all, the man was blind. What else could he want?

Of course, maybe Jesus saw the man's begging bowl. It is possible that other beggars had previously asked the famous healer for money or food rather than healing. But I think there is more to Jesus' question. Samuel Logan Brengle wrote:

Prayer must be definite. Once, when Jesus was leaving Jericho with his disciples and a great number of people, blind Bartimaeus sat by the wayside begging; and when he heard Jesus was passing by, he began to cry out, and say: "Jesus, thou Son of David, have mercy on me." But that prayer was not definite. It was altogether too general. Jesus knew what Bartimaeus wanted, but He desired Bartimaeus to state exactly what he desired, and said to him: "What wilt thou that I should do unto thee?" Then the blind man prayed a definite prayer: "Lord, that I might receive my sight." And the definite prayer there and then received a definite answer, for Jesus said unto him: "Go thy way; thy faith hath made thee whole," and immediately he received his sight (Mark 10:46–52).

We should be as definite when we go to God in asking Him for what we want.[2]

When Jesus taught His followers to pray, He could have told us to pray, "Bless us." He could have used the words, "Provide our needs." He could have said, "Take care of us." But He didn't. He said, "Give us this day our daily bread."[3]

With that word—*bread*—Jesus urged His followers to be specific in prayer.

PRESENT YOUR SPECIFIC NEEDS

But Jesus said to pray for bread. There is no reason to believe He did not mean it literally. To His first followers, bread was central to life. It was a staple. A necessity. A lifeline. So Jesus said, "Pray for bread."

Theologian N. T. Wright wrote:

This clause reminds us that God intends us to pray for specific needs. It is, no doubt, much easier to pray 'God bless everyone' than to pray 'Please bring peace to the Middle East'. It may seem more 'spiritual' to pray for the conversion of the world than for a parking space near to the meeting for which we're about to be late. Now of course we would trivialize Christian prayer if we thought it was only about praying for parking spaces, for our team to win the match, or for fine weather for the church fête. But, once we put the prayer for daily bread within the whole kingdom-prayer where it belongs, to turn then to the specific things we honestly need right now is not trivial. It is precisely what children do when they love and trust the one they call 'Father'.[4]

Praying for specific needs clarifies our minds. I can easily imagine Jesus responding to my prayers as He spoke to Bartimaeus:

"Oh Lord, have mercy on me."

"What do you want Me to do for you?"

"Please come to me."

"What do you want Me to do for you?"

"Please bless me."

"What do you want Me to do for you?"

"Help me."

"What do you want Me to do for you?"

"Well, what I really want is for You to give me the patience or wisdom I need not to scream at my little boy who just spilled his juice all over the new carpet."

"Ah, well, I can do that. I can also remind you to put a lid on his cup from now on."

Now, maybe you don't relate to God in quite that way. But I think that is at least part of what Jesus is urging on us when He teaches us to pray specifically. Jesus' instruction to pray specifically for our needs prompts us to spell out and spill out what we really want to ask.

Praying for specific needs defines our needs. Andrew Murray, in his classic *With Christ in the School of Prayer*, wrote:

> *Our prayers must be a distinct expression of definite need, not a vague appeal to His mercy or an indefinite cry for blessing. It isn't that His loving heart does not understand or is not ready to hear our cry. Rather, Jesus desires such definite prayer for our own sakes because it teaches us to know our own needs better. Time, thought, and self-scrutiny are required to find out what our greatest need really is.[5]*

Often in prayer I have asked God for something and soon have heard myself saying something like, "No, that's not it exactly. It's not *that*, but this other thing I really need." For example, "Lord, bless me" won't lead me to recognize that I don't need a raise as much as I need to say no to buying more stuff or that maybe I don't need a new coworker but the wisdom, love, and humility to resolve my conflicts with the one I have.

Praying for specific needs emphasizes our dependence on and intimacy with God. If I don't really pray for God to provide the bread I need today, I may be tempted to forget that "every good and perfect gift is from above, coming down from the Father."[6] But if I pray for the things I need, I am not only reminded of that fact but also drawn closer to my Father as I do "precisely what children do when they love and trust the one they call 'Father.'"[7]

Praying for specific needs makes us more alert to answers. The other day my sister-in-law Arvilla related how she had purchased several large pieces of furniture in a home furnishings store. After making the purchase, she wheeled the items out to her car on the dolly the store provided. Just then she realized that the furniture would have to be lifted into the back of her SUV. So she prayed. "Lord, You're going to have to either make me stronger or send someone strong enough to help me," she said as she unlocked her vehicle and opened the back. Then she turned around to see a tall, muscular man approaching. She asked for his help, and he gave it and went on his way. Her specific prayer was answered, and because of the way she had prayed, there was no question in her mind that her prayer was answered. If I pray for blessings, God may answer but I may not recognize the answer when it comes. But if, on the other hand, I pray for bread—or "someone strong enough"—I will be more attentive and alert to the answer when it comes. Such prayer, wrote Andrew Murray, "helps us to wait for the special answer and to mark it when it comes."[8]

Praying for specific needs increases our faith. As a young pastor, I was awed by the men and women of faith who surrounded me. Their lives, words, and prayers revealed depths and heights of faith that were simultaneously attractive to me and seemingly impossible for me. Then one day, decades later, I realized that I truly believed and trusted God—probably not as well as those I looked up to years ago but certainly in ways I had once thought impossible. It surprised me and still does. But I thought I knew why. Because in those years I had experienced—over and over again—God's faithfulness in hearing and answering prayer. The more I learned to pray specifically, the more I saw and marked and remembered His answers. And each time that happened, my faith grew.

Confess Your Specific Wants

Praying specifically helps me in many ways as I pray for my needs. But I do not pray only for my needs; I also pray for my wants.

The psalmist David once prayed, "Lord, you know everything I want; my cries are not hidden from you."[9] Commenting on that verse, Charles Haddon Spurgeon said, "Blessed be God, he reads the longings of our hearts; nothing can be hidden from him."[10] Since your Father already knows not only your needs but also your wants, there is no need to be anything but honest in confessing these to God and great advantage in being specific about your wants. To quote Murray again:

> *So much of our prayer is vague and pointless. Some cry for mercy, but do not take the trouble to know exactly why they want it. Others ask to be delivered from sin, but do not name any sin from which a deliverance can be claimed. Still others pray for God's blessing on those around them—for the outpouring of God's Spirit on their land or on the world—and yet have no special field where they can wait and expect to see the answer. To everyone the Lord says, "What do you really want, and what do you expect me to do?"[11]*

What do you want? Praying specifically for your needs not only helps to define your needs but also helps to distinguish them from your wants—which then allows you to confess your wants, knowing of course that they are in a different category from your needs. "God shall supply all your need,"[12] the Bible says, not all your wants. But He also never said He'd stop there.

God already knows everything you want, but confessing your specific desires to Him accomplishes many of the same things as presenting your specific needs to Him. So tell Him. Tell Him you want a different job. Tell Him you want to reconcile with a friend. Tell Him you want new shoes. "You do not have, because you do not ask,"[13] the Bible says, while also warning against greed and selfishness.[14] So do as suggested in an old Gospel song that imagined a phone call to Jesus, and "Tell Him what you want."

SHARE YOUR SPECIFIC FEELINGS

Cain bitterly protested the punishment God gave him for killing his brother, Abel.[15]

The patriarch Abraham complained to God in prayer, lamenting his lack of a son.[16]

Elijah moaned a prayer in depression after an exhausting victory on Mount Carmel, telling God he wanted to die.[17]

King Hezekiah cried bitterly from his sickbed, telling God he *didn't* want to die.[18]

David prayed joyfully to God for not letting King Saul kill him![19]

Habakkuk grumbled about God's inaction.[20]

Samson griped about being thirsty.[21]

Hannah grieved because she was childless.[22]

The Bible depicts people whining, singing, cursing, and grumbling to God. The Bible is filled with prayers that exhibit fear, doubt, joy, anger, hurt, gratitude, confidence, and confusion. By contrast, most if not all of the prayers we hear in most churches or on Christian radio and television are much less emotional and much more uniform. We hear predominantly positive prayers, and even our private prayers tend to be unemotional if not dishonest.

But sharing our feelings with God is certainly included in Jesus' instruction to pray specifically. After all, on the night He was betrayed, He prayed with gut-wrenching, blood-sweating emotion, unloading His anguish without reservation, until an angel had to come to comfort Him.[23]

So when you pray, share your feelings. Be specific about them. Be straightforward. Tell your Father not only what you're thinking, what you need, and what you want, but also what you're feeling. Pour it out. He knows it anyway, but as C. S. Lewis said, we must learn to "lay before Him what is in us, not what ought to be in us."[24]

VOICE YOUR SPECIFIC DREAMS

Some years ago my wife and I teamed up with four friends to start a new church in Oxford, Ohio. For the first seven years of that church's existence, we rented public school space for our worship gatherings. Finally, we were able to purchase land and start construction on a new facility. At the groundbreaking ceremony, we plotted the outline of the building with a few wooden stakes at the corners of each wing. Then we made available a wheelbarrow full of stakes and a bunch of markers. We asked the people at the groundbreaking to take a stake, write on it the name of someone they would like to someday see become a follower of Christ and worship in that place, and drive it into the soil as an act of prayer. One by one, people took stakes and prayerfully wrote on them. Some took several stakes. Some wrote multiple names on a single stake.

It became a precious moment as individuals, couples, families—even small children—marked the outline of that future facility with their hopes and dreams for family members, friends, neighbors, coworkers, and classmates. People huddled together in prayer. Tears streamed down some faces. And moments later, the outline of that future church building not only took shape but also shaped our prayers in the form of our hopes and dreams.

Before Jesus told Bartimaeus "Go, your faith has healed you," He invited him to dream: "What do you want me to do for you?" He called him out of his beggarly posture and into a more active stance. He opened the eyes of his heart and mind before He opened his eyes. He invited Bartimaeus to exercise spiritual vision before He granted him physical vision.

What do *you* want God to do for you? What would you

like to see? Where do you want to be? How would you like to be better? What are your hopes and dreams? Have you ever told them to Jesus? Have you ever voiced them—specifically—to Him?

Why would you ask Jesus to put a little grain in your beggar's bowl when He has the power to heal you? Why not ask for more? Why not go for broke? If you are praying only for things that can realistically happen, you aren't dreaming. If you are reluctant to voice your specific dreams to God, you are missing out.

When you pray, Jesus said, pray for bread. You may not have bread. You may not have the means to get bread. There may be a bread shortage. But don't let any of that stop you. Ask. Dream. Envision. And expect.

Jesus, Son of David, have mercy on me! Teach me and remind me to pray specifically for my needs—for my physical needs (especially _____), my financial needs (especially _____), my relational needs (especially _____), and my spiritual needs (especially _____).

Jesus, Son of David, have mercy on me! I confess to You the things I want. They are not needs, but I sure would like it if You would _____ .

Jesus, Son of David, have mercy on me! Today, right now, I want to get better at sharing my feelings with You. Help me to be honest with myself and with You about what I'm feeling. I ask for Your help in identifying and expressing my specific emotions to You, even right now as I am feeling _____ .

Jesus, Son of David, have mercy on me! Help me to dream and to voice my dreams to You. Save me from misguided timidity, even faithlessness, about the future. Give me faith to tell You what I really want, even in my wildest dreams. Amen.

10

PRAY CONTRITELY

Hoarders was an American reality television series on the A&E network. Each episode of the series, which ran for six seasons (2009–2013), focused on a person who exhibited an obsessive need to collect things—even worthless, dangerous, or unhealthy things—until their homes and lives became utterly unmanageable.

I watched one or two episodes and found it thoroughly depressing as the camera showed room after room piled high with garbage bags, takeout containers, stacks of newspapers, flea market purchases, dirty laundry, collectors' items still in the original packaging, or even—in one case—a freezer filled with the homeowner's deceased cats. The show's hosts—usually a professional therapist and a professional organizer—tiptoed through the chaos and filth with a camera crew before sitting down with the hoarder and discussing the problem. In some cases, the hoarding behavior seemed to originate in a traumatic experience—the death of a spouse, for example. Other catalysts were harder to pin down. But each of the hoarders' obsessive tendencies began somewhere. Every one of those overstuffed rooms was once empty and clean. Every "unmanageable" mountain of junk and trash was once a single McDonald's bag or souvenir that was added to, a little at a time, until the possessions possessed their owner.

That is like the human heart and soul, in some ways. Most of us don't become overburdened all of a sudden. We don't succumb to guilt and shame in one fell swoop. It starts small. With a white lie, perhaps. And then we tell another to cover up the first. We add a little cheating here, a little lusting there. But what was once a solitary sin is added to, a little at a time, until it overwhelms us and weighs us down.

That is why Jesus, in the prayer pattern He recommended to His followers, included the confession of sin. He said, "Pray like this: . . . Forgive us."[1]

A DAILY SOUL-SWEEP

When Jesus modeled prayer to His early followers, He included the confession of sin and request for forgiveness in His short recipe. In doing so, He made it clear that praying contritely is an important part of the red-letter prayer life. That word—*contrite*—is not one we use much these days, but it means both humble and repentant. It is an attitude and a posture God finds attractive, as He told the prophet Isaiah:

> *This is what the high and exalted One says—*
> *he who lives forever, whose name is holy:*
> *"I live in a high and holy place,*
> *but also with the one who is contrite and lowly in spirit,*
> *to revive the spirit of the lowly*
> *and to revive the heart of the contrite."* [2]

That was the attitude Jesus commended in His story of the tax collector and the Pharisee who went into the temple to pray, found in Luke 18:9–14. The Pharisee—an upstanding citizen and religious leader—preened and pontificated in his prayer, while the tax collector confessed his sinfulness and asked for forgiveness, saying, "God, have mercy on me, a sinner"—and thus "went home justified before God."³

The red-letter model for prayer is a daily soul-sweep, one that follows the request for today's bread with a plea for today's pardon. It is a kind of clearing of the daily mess we make, a wise preventive measure that keeps us from hoarding sins to our soul's detriment. It is a daily do-over. A treasure of grace in the single word *forgive*.

ADMIT YOUR HELPLESSNESS

When Jesus depicted the tax collector praying in the temple, He said, "The tax collector, standing far off, would not even lift up his eyes to heaven, but beat his breast, saying, 'God, be merciful to me, a sinner!' "⁴ He did not approach God as someone who had anything to offer but stood "far off." He did not gaze up toward heaven as someone who could face his Maker but "would not even lift up his eyes." He did not stand tall and puff out his chest as someone who could expect some reward or praise but "beat his breast," humbly and brokenly owning his responsibility for his sin.

When Jesus told His followers to pray, "Forgive us our sins," in His model prayer, He was prescribing not only a phrase but an attitude. He is telling us to admit our helplessness. He is urging a humble awareness of our need for mercy and grace. Theologian Karl Barth wrote:

We are God's debtors. We owe him not something, whether it be little or much, but, quite simply, our person in its totality; we owe him ourselves, since we are his creatures, sustained and nourished by his goodness. We, his children, called by his word, admitted to the service of his glorification—we, brothers and sisters of the man Jesus Christ—come short of what we owe to God. What we are and what we do correspond in no wise to what is given us. We are his children and we know not how to recognize it. Calvin says, "Whoever refuses to confess that we offend God, as debtors who do not pay, excludes himself from Christianity." And Luther, "Before God everyone is compelled to lower his plumes."[5]

Praying contritely means lowering our plumes—a reference to the decorative feathers attached to a military headdress, which indicated a soldier's rank or regiment. It means standing "far off," lowering our gaze, and beating our breasts. It means owning our helplessness, our utter lack of right or rank before God.

CONFESS YOUR SIN

According to Jesus, confession is a minimum daily requirement. Praying, "Forgive us," every day will keep the soul swept and the heart uncluttered.

Unfortunately, author and pastor Bill Hybels calls confession "probably the most neglected area in personal prayer today."[6] He wrote:

We often hear people pray publicly, "Lord, forgive us for our many sins." A lot of us carry that approach into our private prayer. We throw all our sins onto a pile without so much as looking at them, and we say, "God, please cover the whole dirty heap."

This approach to confession, unfortunately, is a
colossal cop-out. When I lump all my sins together and
confess them en masse, it's not too painful or embarrassing.
But if I take those sins out of the pile one by one and call
them by name, it's a whole new ball game.

I determined that in my prayers, I would deal with
sin specifically. I would say, "I told so-and-so there were
nine hundred cars in the parking lot when really there
were only six hundred. That was a lie, and therefore I
am a liar. I plead for your forgiveness for being a liar."

Or instead of admitting I had been less than the best
husband, I would say, "Today I willfully determined
to be self-centered, uncaring and insensitive. It was a
calculated decision. I walked through the door thinking,
'I'm not going to serve her tonight. I had a hard day,
and I deserve to have things my way.' I need your
forgiveness for the sin of selfishness."[7]

In my evening prayers, I will often pray a confession based on
the words of the Book of Common Prayer: "Almighty God,
my Father, I confess that I have sinned against You through my
own fault, in thought, word, and deed, in what I have done
and in what I have left undone." I will then go back and review
my day phrase by phrase: "In thought, I harbored bitterness
toward that person in the store. I lusted. . .I doubted. . ." and
so on, ending with a review of things I left undone that I
should have done, such as the apology I didn't offer or the
coworker's misstatement I didn't correct because it made me
look better than I would have otherwise.

This may seem a bit too introspective. It may sound

negative. But daily confession is actually a blessing, a boon to our souls. For the follower of Jesus, Roger L. Ray writes,

> *it is only the unconfessed sin that can hurt us. It is the unacknowledged, the denied and excused aspects of our lives that force us to lie about ourselves to ourselves and to others. The moment we can acknowledge a sin, recovery begins. . . . When we are willing to recognize our hostility, our resentment, our anger, lust, greed, and self-centeredness, we find the hope for a new way of being.*[8]

As the old adage goes, "Confession is good for the soul." So pray contritely.

ACCEPT GOD'S FORGIVENESS

It was not only a daily confession that Jesus commended to His followers but also a daily cleansing. As the beloved disciple, John, would later write, "If we confess our sins, he is faithful and just to forgive us our sins and to cleanse us from all unrighteousness."[9] Our confession opens the door to the willing forgiveness of our Father.

Philip Keller wrote:

> *"Forgive us our debts" may well be the four most important words that ever cross our lips, provided we really mean them. Any man, any woman who comes to our Father in heaven with a genuine, heartfelt attitude of contrition is bound to find forgiveness. There will fall from the shoulders the old burden of guilt, and, in its place, there will be wrapped around our hearts a*

*radiant sense of warmth, affection, love, and acceptance.
"You are forgiven. You are mine. You do belong. You are
home!"*

*This is the reception which the Father gave the
prodigal son when he came home asking forgiveness.
Little did he realize, all the time he was away from his
home and his father, he was a forgiven man. Little did
he know that, despite his misconduct, his father's love
and concern for him had never diminished. Little did
he recognize the yearning outreach of his father's heart
toward him, even when his behavior besmirched and
shamed the family name.*

*This is perhaps the most poignant picture portrayed
for us in all of Scripture depicting the loving forgiveness
of our Father. The son's forgiveness was not contingent
upon a change of conduct or his making a fresh
resolution to behave better, or even upon his sense
of remorse and contrition. His forgiveness was freely
bestowed and gladly given simply because he had come,
willing to admit his wrong and accept pardon. The very
character of God our Father can do no less than extend
this sort of total and complete forgiveness to all who turn
to Him for it.*[10]

Some people, however, struggle to receive God's forgiveness
because they cannot forgive themselves. A friend of mine
tearfully confessed that he could never forgive himself for
something he had done. I listened and then said something
without thinking (I hate it when that happens. . .and I often
wish it would happen less frequently than it does): "Wow," I

said, "you must have really high standards."

He blinked at me through his tears. "What do you mean?"

"Well, you believe God can and will and does forgive even the worst sinner, right?"

"Right." The word came out slowly, as though he suspected a trap.

"But *you* can't forgive *yourself.*"

He nodded. "Right."

"Which seems to indicate that your standards are higher than those of the holy, righteous God of the universe."

He blinked some more.

"Which maybe—I'm just spit-balling here—says that either you or your sin is bigger in your mind than God is."

He shook his head. "No, I—I'm not saying that."

"But if God says you're forgiven, and you say what you did is unforgivable. . .you both can't be right. So it really sounds like you're saying you know more than God. Or your standards are higher than God's. Or maybe *you* are."

He didn't answer but continued to shake his head.

I tried again. "I think the issue is whether you can accept what God says instead of what you think—whether you can believe that God's mercy and grace are bigger than your sin and guilt, whether you can really trust His promise that if you confess your sins He will forgive your sin and cleanse you from all unrighteousness."

It took some more time and discussion, but before we were done talking, his resistance melted away, and he was able to accept God's forgiveness.

When we pray, "Forgive us," we can accept the Father's forgiveness and claim His cleansing work in our hearts. We can leave our past in our past. We can check our baggage and walk away unencumbered. We can experience the blessing expressed by hymn writer Albert Orsborn:

> *Wash from my hands the dust of earthly striving;*
> *Take from my mind the stress of secret fear;*
> *Cleanse Thou the wounds from all but Thee far hidden.*
> *And when the waters flow let my healing appear.* [11]

DO IT AGAIN TOMORROW

Just as Jesus intended for His followers to pray for daily bread, He aimed for them to make a daily confession and experience a daily cleansing when He told them to pray, "Forgive us our sins." It is a necessary and progressive exercise.

It is necessary because, as the Spirit of God works in us and refines us, we may experience deliverance from sins that once "so easily beset us." [12] Praying contritely—sincerely and specifically confronting the sins we have committed—not only increases our awareness of our weakness but also heightens our awareness of our need for God's moment-by-moment presence and power in our daily lives.

It is a progressive exercise because while we are experiencing victory in one area, the Spirit will shine a light on another area. Things we might never have noticed a year ago suddenly become a focus of our conviction and confession. As we grow in grace, we grow in sensitivity to sin.

Shakespeare seems to have known this. In his play *Hamlet*—considered by many to be his finest work—he inserted a scene in act 3 in which Prince Hamlet pleads with his mother to turn from her scandalous relationship with her late husband's brother. He begs her:

> *Confess yourself to heaven;*
> *Repent what's past; avoid what is to come. . . .*
> *Refrain to-night,*
> *And that shall lend a kind of easiness*
> *To the next abstinence: the next more easy;*
> *For use almost can change the stamp of nature,*
> *And either master the devil or throw him out*
> *With wondrous potency.* [13]

In plainer English, Hamlet's point was that repenting and refraining from sin can make it easier to refrain tomorrow, and even easier the next day. In that way, "use" or practice can "change the stamp of nature," transforming a habit that once seemed "natural."

Praying contritely means admitting your helplessness, confessing your sin, accepting God's forgiveness, and then doing it again tomorrow. And the next day. As you "pray like this,"[14] you will wash from your hands "the dust of earthly striving," take from your mind "the stress of secret fear," cleanse from your heart the wounds of hidden sins, and see in your life the healing streams appear.[15]

> *Almighty God, my Father,*
> *I make that my prayer.*
> *Grant me the grace of daily confession, daily*
> *forgiveness, and daily cleansing.*
> *Wash from my hands the dust of earthly striving.*
> *Make me sensitive to sin's approach.*

Make me quick to confess my sins to You.
Let me daily experience Your forgiveness and
cleansing, and let me walk in newness of life
to the glory of Your name, amen.

11

PRAY GRACIOUSLY

~

I t sounds like something out of a horror movie, but it's real. In recent years, scientists have discovered a kind of bacterial infection called necrotizing fasciitis, more commonly called flesh-eating bacteria. Once this bacterium enters a human body, it can multiply rapidly. Within twenty-four hours, its victim begins to experience flu-like symptoms, severe thirst, and extreme weakness. Within three to four days, the limb or area of the body most affected will begin to swell, and dark blisters filled with blackish fluid will appear. At five days, the victim's blood pressure will drop severely, and he or she will go into toxic shock.

If it's not discovered early and treated quickly and aggressively, it can consume a person's health and well-being from the inside out and eventually take that person's life.

If you read that description and started to feel a little queasy or worry that you might have necrotizing fasciitis, you can probably relax (though you may want to talk to someone about your hypochondriac tendencies). Necrotizing fasciitis is fairly rare, fewer than a thousand cases a year in the United States, for example.

But necrotizing fasciitis has its parallel in the spiritual realm, and just like its physical counterpart, this spiritual affliction can fester and grow. If it's not discovered early and treated quickly and aggressively, it can consume a person's spirit and soul from the inside out and eventually rob that person of his or her spiritual life and vitality.

My wife, the lovely Robin, once ran into that malady in an office setting with five or six other women. They were all accomplished. They were all avowed followers of Jesus. And with just one or two exceptions, they were bitter and unkind people.

Robin was often stung by their cutting and condescending remarks to her and about her. She was the youngest in the group and wanted to look up to those women and learn from them and more than once wondered what she was doing wrong and how she might be more accepted and more esteemed by the other women in her department.

Part of Robin's responsibility in the office was to design, plan, and host various events and banquets. She has always been gifted in hospitality and adept at pulling off large, successful events. However, on more than one occasion, after she had arranged centerpieces and set an elegant table, she witnessed one of her coworkers follow behind her and rearrange things to her liking—only to be surreptitiously followed by yet another woman who rearranged everything according to her preferences! It was funny, when it stopped being irritating.

One day she came to me with tears in her eyes after some new insult or reproach. She could easily have blamed her coworkers and vowed to get even. She could have written them off. She could have decided to beat them at their own game. But she did none of those things.

"They're so bitter and angry," she said. "They're still hurting over things that happened years ago, things they've never forgiven, never let go of. Promise me that if you see me holding on to things like that, you'll tell me. I don't want to become a bitter, unhappy old woman."

I'm happy to report that, though several decades have passed since she asked me to make that promise, she's avoided infection. And the antidote for her—as it is for any of us—was prescribed by Jesus in the prayer He taught His disciples when He told them to pray, "Forgive us as we forgive."[1]

THE BIGGEST TWO-LETTER WORD

When Jesus taught His followers to pray, He linked the petition for daily bread with the petition for forgiveness:

> *"Give us this day our daily bread,*
> *and forgive us our debts,*
>   *as we also have forgiven our debtors."* [2]

I think it was intentional. I think both the plea for bread and the prayer for forgiveness are supposed to be daily requests because we need both, every day: food and forgiveness. We should pray for both, every day. We will grow as we experience both, every day.

But notice also that Jesus linked our forgiveness from God with our forgiveness of others. "Forgive us," He told us to pray, "*as* we forgive."

"As we forgive."

As.

That has to be the biggest two-letter word imaginable. Forgive us *as* we forgive. It can be taken several different ways. And that may be intentional, too, because each of the possible meanings contained in that little word is instructive and potentially life changing.

PRAY TO FORGIVE WILLINGLY

When Jesus says, "Pray like this. . . . Forgive us as we forgive," He teaches us to pray graciously. He also teaches us that our forgiveness of others somehow activates the Father's forgiveness of us.

"Forgive us *as* we forgive others." That phrase can be taken to mean "Forgive us *in the same way* we forgive others." It can be understood as a suggestion that our forgiveness of others will set the tone for the Father's forgiveness of us.

Jesus said as much. After He taught His model prayer to His first followers, He did what most rabbis would do—He offered a little commentary. And while He could have chosen to comment on the use of the plural *our* or His address of God as Father or the request for bread, He didn't. Even though He ended His prayer with the request for deliverance from evil, He rewound things a bit and commented on the prayer for forgiveness:

> *"For if you forgive others their trespasses, your heavenly Father will also forgive you, but if you do not forgive others their trespasses, neither will your Father forgive your trespasses."*[3]

Wow. I don't know how He could be any more straightforward. On another occasion, Jesus told a parable to get across the same point:

> *"The kingdom of heaven may be compared to a king who wished to settle accounts with his servants. When he began to settle, one was brought to him who owed him*

ten thousand talents. And since he could not pay, his master ordered him to be sold, with his wife and children and all that he had, and payment to be made. So the servant fell on his knees, imploring him, 'Have patience with me, and I will pay you everything.' And out of pity for him, the master of that servant released him and forgave him the debt. But when that same servant went out, he found one of his fellow servants who owed him a hundred denarii, and seizing him, he began to choke him, saying, 'Pay what you owe.' So his fellow servant fell down and pleaded with him, 'Have patience with me, and I will pay you.' He refused and went and put him in prison until he should pay the debt. When his fellow servants saw what had taken place, they were greatly distressed, and they went and reported to their master all that had taken place. Then his master summoned him and said to him, 'You wicked servant! I forgave you all that debt because you pleaded with me. And should not you have had mercy on your fellow servant, as I had mercy on you?' And in anger his master delivered him to the jailers, until he should pay all his debt. So also my heavenly Father will do to every one of you, if you do not forgive your brother from your heart."[4]

Wow again. Jesus didn't mince words. I don't know how He could make it any clearer: forgiveness is a big deal.

And it's a big deal not primarily because it's bad for the people we can't or won't forgive; it's a big deal because it's bad for us. It's a soul-eating infection. It will eat away at us from the inside out, and it will short-circuit our experience of forgiveness.

James Mulholland, in *Praying Like Jesus,* wrote:

> *"Forgive us our sins as we forgive those who sin against
> us" is such a clever phrase. In one sentence, it reminds
> us of so much. We have sinned. . . . We need forgiveness.
> Others have sinned against us. They need forgiveness.
> Our Father is a forgiving God. We need to be as
> forgiving. The Prayer of Jesus asks this question: Do we
> want God's forgiveness to be diminished or our mercy to
> be expanded? Do we want God to use human measures?*[5]

That's it, exactly. Jesus teaches us to pray for our mercy to be
expanded. The answer to our prayers is implicit in the prayer
itself. "Forgive us *as* we forgive others."

I don't want God to forgive me grudgingly. I don't want
Him to torture me or toy with me. I want Him to forgive
me willingly. I want Him to run to me as the father of the
prodigal raced to his son, meeting him, embracing him, even
interrupting his confession with grace![6]

So when I pray, "Forgive us *as* we forgive others," I am
saying I want my mercy to be expanded. I want to forgive
willingly because that's the kind of reception I want from
God. I don't want God to measure out my forgiveness in
measly human ways; I want to measure out forgiveness to
others in big ol' God ways. I want to be willing to forgive. I
want to be quick to forgive. I want to turn that phrase from
the Lord's Prayer around and "forgive others as God forgives
me," which is exactly what Paul later wrote to the Christians
in Colosse: "Bear with each other and forgive one another

if any of you has a grievance against someone. Forgive as the Lord forgave you." [7]

PRAY TO FORGIVE FULLY

The words "Forgive us *as* we forgive" may also be taken to mean "Forgive us *to the extent* that we forgive others." None of us wants partial forgiveness from God, so we pray for grace to forgive fully, because that is how God forgives—and what we need.

Jesus' parable in Matthew 18 has as its main character a king and one of his servants. But when Jesus called this man a servant, he didn't mean a butler, gardener, court jester, or anything along those lines. The picture he painted was of a high official, a budget director or chief financial officer or secretary of the treasury—an important man who handled large sums of money.

And Jesus depicts that man as owing an enormous sum, a gargantuan amount. In a day when the gross national product of the entire province of Galilee was only three hundred talents, Jesus chose an unimaginably high debt. If he were telling this story today, he might use the late Carl Sagan's signature phrase to say the man owed "*billions* and *billions*" of dollars.

But, Jesus says, since he was not able to pay, "his master ordered him to be sold, with his wife and children and all that he had, and payment to be made." [8] That was how such a debt was met in those days. Rather than filing for bankruptcy as we do now, it was common in ancient times for a man and his family and possessions to be sold for such a debt.

So the servant did what I would do—what you would do, I imagine:

So the servant fell on his knees, imploring him, "Have patience with me, and I will pay you everything." And out of pity for him, the master of that servant released him and forgave him the debt.[9]

Now, something important is happening in the details of Jesus' story. I just love Jesus' mastery of nuance when He tells a story; He did it all the time, and He does it in this story, too. Notice that the servant begged for time: "Have patience with me, and I will pay you everything."

But the king did not give him an extension, as he had asked. What did the king do?

Jesus said the king "forgave him the debt"!

Don't miss that detail. It's key. The servant asked for a chance to make things right, but the king canceled the debt. The servant begged for a little mercy, but the king gave him immeasurable grace. The servant pleaded for a little wiggle room, but the king granted him complete amnesty.

That is a picture of how those who have experienced new life in Christ have been forgiven. We begged for mercy and received grace. We bartered for help and received the Helper. We asked for heart medicine and received a heart transplant.

Key to the ability to forgive is the grace to grasp the reality, the depth, the height, the extent of our own forgiveness, of how much and how completely we have been forgiven.

Unfortunately, we are too often like the servant in Jesus' parable, who went out, found someone who owed him a pittance, a hundred denarii, less than twenty lousy bucks, and rather than forgiving as he had been forgiven, demanded immediate payment in full.

Despite the incredible debt that has been willingly, graciously, generously canceled for us, we withhold mercy (let alone grace), harbor a grudge, and nurse bitterness in our hearts toward someone who has hurt us.

And like flesh-eating bacteria, that unforgiveness is causing more damage to us, to our hearts, our spirits, than to anyone else. In fact, according to Jesus' parable, somehow God will take His cue. . .from you. He wants your mercy to be expanded, but if you choose instead to limit His forgiveness, He will not overrule your wishes. He will "forgive us *as* we forgive."

For some of us, that will mean we must face the wrong that's been done to us. Some of us run so hard and fast from conflict that we don't want to face the fact that someone hurt us. Maybe because that means admitting that Mom and Dad weren't perfect. Maybe because it feels wrong somehow to admit that my husband is an abuser or my friend acted selfishly or my pastor did something wrong or that God Himself disappointed me. Maybe because I am not about to give that person the satisfaction of knowing he or she hurt me or maybe because if I face the wrong that was done I might have to pursue biblical reconciliation, and I don't want to. It scares me, or it's too much work, perhaps.

But if I'm going to avoid the soul-eating cancer of unforgiveness in my life, I've got to face the wrong that's been done to me.

Not only that, but for some of us, the process of

forgiving someone who has wronged us will mean facing *our* responsibility. It may mean coming to grips with the part *we* may have played—any wrongs we may have committed— toward the person who hurt us. It may mean facing the fact that the hurt we *don't* deserve is mixed in with some hurt we *do* deserve! It may mean facing the need to forgive ourselves as a first step toward forgiving someone else.

But God commands us to forgive, and He never commands us to do something we have no control over. So forgiving means to decide, to will, to let go of the wrong that has been done to us, to throw out the scorecard, to erase the debt.

Does that sound too hard? It can be hard. But sometimes it helps to make a symbolic gesture that will help bring your emotions into line with your will. Like writing down the wrongs you choose to forgive and then burning them as a way of letting them go. Or prayerfully placing all those offenses on a paper boat and sending it off down a stream until it disappears from your sight. Or burying a hatchet, the way some American tribes did—just don't mark the spot so you can come back later and dig it up!

For some reason we think that withholding forgiveness is going to make us feel better. . .even though we've been withholding forgiveness, and withholding, and withholding, and yet we're still miserable, still struggling, still flailing, still trying to move on, still trying to figure out why we can't get better and even seem to be getting worse, as if something keeps eating away at our happiness and our hope and our spiritual strength.

But maybe, just maybe, if we can grasp the reality of our own forgivenness and grant forgiveness to those who hurt us, we can actually move down the path toward healing. Maybe healing comes as we learn to pray, "Forgive us *as* we forgive." And maybe forgiving fully opens the door to healing fully.

If "Forgive us *as* we forgive" means "Forgive us *to the same extent* that we forgive," then how much mercy and grace and beauty will flow to us and through us as we learn to forgive fully, the way we wish to be forgiven?

PRAY TO FORGIVE CONSTANTLY

Those weighty words of the prayer Jesus taught His followers—"Forgive us *as* we forgive"—have one more thing to teach us. That little word *as* can also be taken to mean "while." That is, it is possible to understand that prayer to mean "Forgive us *while we are in the act* of forgiving those who sin against us."

You see, when God forgives, it's a done deal. The Bible says when He forgives, He forgets. He says in Jeremiah 50:20 that when He forgives His people's sins, no amount of searching will ever find them again.

The bad news is: we are not like that. Very often, with us, forgiveness is not so simple or so complete. Often, with us, forgiveness must be a daily decision.

But the good news is this: forgiveness can be a daily decision. Remember, Jesus structured His model prayer to include the prayer for forgiveness in the same breath as the prayer for daily bread. So just as we pray for daily bread, we pray for daily forgiveness.

"Forgive us *as* we forgive." In other words, "Forgive us today as we are forgiving today."

If the enemy of your soul, the devil, whispers in your

ear and reminds you what so-and-so did, you can choose—today—to grasp the reality of your own forgivenness and extend that same mercy to whoever hurt you. You don't have to feel like it. You don't have to gin up any warm feelings for that person. But you can refuse to retaliate today. You can wipe the slate clean today. You can forgive that debt today. You can pray, "Forgive us today as we are forgiving today."

And as you do that, day by day, week by week, month by month, the forgivenness that accompanies your forgiveness will place a growing distance between you and the thing you've forgiven, like setting a toy boat into a flowing stream or river. Once you release the boat into the current, it will be taken farther and farther away until, sometime in the future, you'll lose sight of it.

And it will lose hold of you.

Lord Jesus, You say so much in just a few words.

You teach me to forgive, even as You show me how much I have to learn.

You remind me how much I've been forgiven and how much mercy and grace have been showered on me, and then You invite me to be like that.

I can be like that? I can forgive as I have been forgiven?

As willingly?

As fully?

As constantly?

You must mean it because You command it.

If You command it, You can do it, in me and through me.

So I pray, forgive me as I forgive others.
I want my mercy to be expanded until it is like
Yours. I want my forgiving to echo Yours. I want Your
grace and kindness to flow through me. . .even to those
who have hurt me, who have sinned against me.
Forgive me as I forgive.
Amen.

12

PRAY SUBMISSIVELY

—

I like to be in control.

Maybe you do, too. But my need for control is probably greater than yours. (I also tend to be pretty competitive.)

Nearly twenty years ago, my wife and I were enjoying a marriage retreat with several other couples. We ate and laughed and cried together throughout the various sessions, which were brilliantly led by professional facilitators, a married couple. As part of the retreat, Robin and I were each given a diagnostic tool, a survey, to fill out. I don't recall all the things the survey was supposed to diagnose. But she and I both remember the facilitators' reactions when they sat down with the two of us, our surveys in their hands.

"How long have you two been married?" the husband asked.

Robin and I exchanged glances and answered, almost in unison, "Twenty-two years."

"Has it been difficult?" the wife asked.

The looks we exchanged before answering were mostly puzzled. "Not at all," I said.

"We've had our ups and downs," Robin said, "like anyone. But it's been wonderful. Why, is something wrong?"

The facilitators shook their heads. "No," the husband answered. "It's just—well, we've just never seen results like these in a successful marriage."

That sounded ominous. "What do you mean?" I asked.

He smiled, shaking his head again. "You both scored very high in 'control.'"

That was surprising to neither of us. We smiled at each other.

He continued, "Usually in a marriage, one partner scores high in the need for control while the other is much lower. You know, to one person control is very important, but the other person in the marriage is more. . ."

"Agreeable?" I offered.

He smiled. "Laid back. But you two scored a ninety-seven and ninety-five in 'control,' on a scale of one hundred."

"That sounds about right," Robin said.

"Which is which?" I asked.

"The more important question," the wife said, "is how do you do it?" She explained that two people who place such a high value on control would almost certainly butt heads so regularly as to make a marriage extremely contentious.

My wife and I laughed, and she mentioned that not only had we enjoyed a happy, successful marriage for more than two decades, but we had also worked in ministry together— sometimes with adjoining desks—for much of that time. To my suggestion that we were simply exceptional people, Robin offered a more likely answer, telling our retreat leaders that we had managed to divide roles and tasks according to our individual gifts and preferences, so that we exercised control in our own specific areas and deferred to the other in his or her's.

You may not like—or need—to be in control as much as me or my wife, but most of us prefer more control to less, which can be a problem when we pray. Jesus knows this, of course.

FROM PARTNERSHIP TO PETITION

When Jesus taught His followers to pray, He first delivered to them a three-part petition that would align them with God's reputation, kingdom, and will:

"Hallowed be Your name.
Your kingdom come.
Your will be done
On earth as it is in heaven." [1]

Next, He taught them to turn their thoughts and prayers toward themselves and their needs in what can be understood as another three-part petition:

"Give us this day our daily bread,
and forgive us our debts,
*   as we also have forgiven our debtors.*
And lead us not into temptation,
*   but deliver us from evil."* [2]

I know I'm not the sharpest tack in the carpet, but I can see the brilliance in Jesus' progression of thought. He seems to understand that most of us like to control things. We are usually reluctant to surrender control and seek God's leadership in our lives. So He doesn't begin His prayer with an act of surrender but an acknowledgment of our relationship with God. Then He teaches us to align ourselves with God's reputation, kingdom, and will in prayer, because prayer is not about getting things from God but partnering with Him. And then, once we do that, He tells us to present our most basic needs to God—to be fed and to be both forgiven and forgiving.

Only after all that does Jesus teach us to ask to be led. Though some Bible versions translate the third petition as something like, "And don't lead us into temptation," I think it is preferable to use the wording some of us memorized from older Bibles: "And lead us not into temptation." One reason is that such phrasing preserves the poetry of the petition, contrasting "lead us not into temptation" with "but deliver us from evil." But another reason I prefer "And lead us not into temptation" is because when I pray the Lord's Prayer—often several times a day—I pause after the words *and lead us*. I make it a prayer of submission before it becomes a prayer for deliverance.

PRAY TO BE LED (AND PRAY FOR GRACE TO FOLLOW)

Give. Forgive. Lead.

Three simple requests. But each has profound effects. And each may have been rich with allusion in the mind of Jesus and in the minds of His earliest students in prayer.

When Jesus said, "Give us this day our daily bread," He and His listeners probably couldn't have helped but remember the experience of their ancestors in the wilderness, when they complained of hunger and God answered with manna, saying, "In the morning you shall be filled with bread. Then you shall know that I am the LORD your God."[3]

When Jesus told them next to pray, "Forgive us," those words may have evoked their collective memory of Israel's impatience and complaining—still, after having been provided manna day by day—that prompted a scourge of "fiery serpents" in the camp that prompted grief, sorrow, repentance, and prayers for forgiveness and healing. . .which were answered when Moses lifted up in their midst a "bronze serpent" on a pole.[4]

Similarly, when Jesus said to pray, "And lead us," He and His hearers may have recalled the pillar of cloud by day and pillar of fire by night—the GPS system by which God led His people out of Egypt and through the wilderness, step by step, turn by turn, until they crossed the Jordan and entered the Promised Land.

So pray to be led like that, and pray also for the grace, wisdom, and courage to follow. Pray, "Lead me along the path of everlasting life."[5] Pray, "Lead me in the right path."[6] Pray, "Lead me in your truth and teach me."[7] Pray, "Lead me to the rock that is higher than I."[8] Pray, "Teach me to do your will, for you are my God! Let your good Spirit lead me on level ground!"[9]

In the words of hymn writer Joseph Gilmore, pray:

Lord, I would place my hand in Thine,
Nor ever murmur nor repine;
Content, whatever lot I see,
Since 'tis my God that leadeth me. [10]

PRAY TO NOT BE LED INTO TRIALS AND TEMPTATIONS

Just as the petitions "Give us," "forgive us," and "lead us" probably prompted memories of Israel's wilderness wanderings, the request to "lead us not into temptation" may have evoked Jesus' own wilderness experience, when according to the Gospel writer Matthew, "Jesus was led up by the Spirit into the wilderness to be tempted by the devil."[11]

It seems nearly impossible to imagine that Jesus would have uttered those words without recalling—and maybe even shuddering at the memory of—his clash with the devil after forty days of fasting and solitude. It would be completely understandable for Jesus—who on at least one other occasion told His closest followers, "Pray that you won't be tempted"[12]— to tell His followers to pray to *not* go through anything like what He endured in the desert after His baptism.

Philip Keller wrote:

> *It had been an agonizing, exacting ordeal from which He emerged totally triumphant. Yet it was a test of such magnitude that we read, "Angels came and ministered unto him" (Mt 4:11). After this conquest of His archenemy, He well knew temptation was a strenuous trial for anyone to face.*
>
> *No doubt, then, one of the reasons He included this petition in the prayer was a compassionate concern for His followers. Being touched with the feeling of our infirmities, He shrank from seeing us exposed to the sort of temptation He Himself had endured.*[13]

But when the Gospel writers Matthew and Luke recorded Jesus' words, "Lead us not into temptation,"[14] they used a Greek word, *peirasmos*, which can also mean trial, calamity, or affliction. For example, it is the word Jesus used during His last supper with the Twelve, when He told them, "You are those who have stayed with me in my trials"[15] (*peirasmos*)— meaning the low points of His life and ministry to that point.

So pray, "Lead us. . .not into temptation." Ask not to be led into a wilderness of temptation. Ask for His help in avoiding sin—in evading even the temptation to sin. Ask the Father to keep you as far from temptation as possible. But ask also to avoid trials and afflictions, big and small, from cancer to flat tires. Just as you ask for daily bread and daily forgiveness, ask for daily avoidance of bad stuff, whether it is a toothache or a tidal wave. You may not avoid every temptation or trial you pray to avoid. You also can't know how many misfortunes your prayers could have averted. Speaking only for myself, I'd rather pray daily not to be led into trials and temptations and let God, in His love and wisdom, answer according to His reputation, kingdom, and will.

PRAY TO BE LED, EVEN IF IT MEANS SUFFERING

The Gospel of Luke records the following event on the night before Jesus' death by crucifixion:

> *And he came out and went, as was his custom, to the Mount of Olives, and the disciples followed him. And when he came to the place, he said to them, "Pray that you may not enter into temptation." And he withdrew from them about a stone's throw, and knelt down and prayed, saying, "Father, if you are willing, remove this cup from me. Nevertheless, not my will, but yours, be done." And there appeared to him an angel from heaven, strengthening him.*[16]

Jesus, who earlier had taught His followers to pray, "Lead us not into *peirasmos*" (into temptation and trial), once again told them to pray against temptation. . .before He withdrew to pray not to be led into the most intense trial He had ever faced. In fact, Matthew's account says that Jesus asked *three times* to escape the coming trial.[17]

And He had to face it anyway.

We are never told exactly how and when Jesus heard the Father say no. Was it an audible answer after His third request? Did the angel deliver the news before offering the necessary comfort and strength? Did Jesus figure it out when He heard the crowd coming to arrest Him? We don't know. We only know that His request, "not my will, but yours, be done," was granted, while "remove this cup from me" was not.

Jesus' words teach us to pray, "Lead us not into temptation." His example teaches us to trust God's good, pleasing, and perfect will[18] even when it means suffering. We must pray to be led, even though it means being led to the cross.

Theologian N. T. Wright pointed out:

> *'My child', says the wise old Jewish writer Ben-Sira (2.1), 'If you come to the Lord, prepare yourself for testing.' . . . To say 'lead us not into temptation'. . . .means 'Enable us to pass safely through the testing of our faith'. Enable us, in other words, to hear the words of Annunciation and, though trembling, to say: Behold, the handmaid of the Lord. Thy will be done; deliver us from evil. We are thus to become people in whose lives the joy and pain of the whole world meet together once more, so that God's new world may at length come to birth.*
>
> *This will mean different things for each of us, as we*

*each grapple with our own testing and temptation. But,
as we do so, we are caught up into something bigger than
ourselves. We are part of that great movement whereby the
hopes and fears of all the years are brought together and
addressed by the living God. And, as we hear that gentle
and powerful address to our own hopes and fears, we are
called to become in our turn, the means whereby that
same address goes out to the wider world. We are called to
pray alongside Mary as she offers herself, her joy and her
pain, for the salvation of the world; alongside the disciples
as, muddled and sleepy, they struggle and fail to pray with
Jesus; above all, alongside Jesus himself, as he weeps in
Gethsemane and staggers on to Calvary.*[19]

Pray to be led. Pray to be led even if it means stress and strain and suffering, and it will. It may be a furnace like that which the three Hebrews endured, or a field of battle, such as the one where David triumphed over Goliath. It may be a throne room (like Esther) or a dungeon (like Daniel). It may be a garden and a scourge and a cross, such as Jesus endured. But pray to be led, nonetheless. "By waters still, over troubled sea," in the words of Joseph Gilmore, let it be the Father's hand "that leadeth me."[20]

PRAY TO BE LED ALL THE WAY TO YOUR LAST BREATH

Jesus tried to warn His closest followers. He told Simon Peter in the upper room, "Satan has asked to sift all of you as wheat. But I have prayed for you, Simon, that your faith may not fail. And when you have turned back, strengthen your brothers."[21]

He forewarned Peter that he would deny Jesus.

He told Peter, James, and John in the garden of Gethsemane, "Watch and pray that you may not enter into temptation."[22]

Yet, Matthew records, "all the disciples left him and fled."[23]

And all of it happened after Jesus taught them to pray, "Lead us not into temptation." Maybe if they had stayed awake in the garden, praying that prayer, they wouldn't have failed so miserably.

I don't want to be like that. I want to be led by the Father moment by moment, day by day, until I exhale my last breath. I want to be like my Rabbi who, hanging naked and battered and bruised on a cross, somehow lifted Himself on his nail-pierced feet and summoned enough strength to call out in a loud voice—not a whimper, but a shout—"Father, into your hands I commit my spirit!"[24]

Pray, "Lead us not into temptation. . .or trial." But pray to be led even if it means suffering. Pray to be led all the way until your last breath, when you can shout, "Father, into Your hands I commit my spirit!" Pray, right now, with Joseph Gilmore:

And when my task on earth is done,
When by Thy grace the vict'ry's won,
E'en death's cold wave I will not flee,
Since God through Jordan leadeth me.[25]

Lord, I pray to be led by You. Give me the grace,
wisdom, and courage to follow.

Teach me to pray, "Lead us not into temptation."
Not into trial. Not into failure or defeat.
Lead me away from temptation.
Lead me away from temptation that would be too
much for me to bear.
Lead me far away from temptation that would
cause my faith to fail.
Lead me far from trial, affliction, and calamity.
Lead me along the path of everlasting life.[26] *Lead*
me in the right path.[27] *Lead me in Your truth and teach*
me.[28] *Lead me to the rock that is higher than I.*[29] *Let*
Your good Spirit lead me on level ground![30]
Lead me all the way from earth to heaven, in Jesus'
name, amen.

13

PRAY PURPOSEFULLY

—

Two of my dearest friends in the world, Dave and Becky, told me the amazing story of their mission trip some years ago to the mountain town of San Luis, Honduras, in the wake of Hurricane Fifi. They traveled as part of a combined medical-and-evangelistic team that served the people's medical and spiritual needs with clinics and evangelistic services.

One night soon after their arrival, Dave and Becky lay down to sleep on a couple of air mattresses in the back of a pickup truck covered with an old camper shell top. Suddenly, Becky heard a sound, like a snap or a click.

She elbowed her husband. "What's that?"

"It's just an animal," Dave answered. He flipped on the flashlight and sat up. He pointed the light out the tiny camper top window and looked out but saw nothing. He told Becky that everything looked quiet. He shut off the light and lay back down.

A few seconds passed, and they heard the sound again.

"There it is again," Becky said.

"There are animals out there, Becky," he said, letting the irritation he felt creep into his voice. It had been a long, tiring day, after all, and they both just wanted to sleep. Becky accepted his assurances, and they both eventually fell asleep.

They finished the successful mission trip and returned home. Three months later, the missionary who had hosted them was back in the United States on furlough and had come to a nearby church to speak. Dave and Becky went to see him.

After the service, when the missionary saw them and greeted them, he said he wanted to talk to them. He led them to a private room and told them to sit down. "I have a story to tell you," he said.

He said that a few months after the mission team left San Luis, he returned to hold more evangelistic services there. One night, as he finished preaching and invited his listeners to come to the front for prayer, three men walked forward together and surrendered their lives to Jesus Christ. Afterward, one of the men stood in front of the congregation and told his story. He said that a few months earlier, when a group of *gringos* had come to San Luis from America, he and his two friends had been drinking at the local cantina. The more they drank, the angrier they became at the outsiders who had invaded their town.

"I got my gun," the man said. "I went to where the gringos were staying. I saw a truck camper and was going to shoot whoever was sleeping in that camper. I snuck up to it and looked in the window. I saw a couple lying inside. I pointed my gun through the window at the man's head and pulled the trigger. But the gun misfired."

He continued, "I heard them talking inside the truck and then a light came on. I ducked under the window and crouched against the side of the truck until the light went off. Then I stood and looked in the window again. I aimed at the man's head and pulled the trigger. It misfired a second time! When that happened, suddenly a rush of fear came over me, and I ran away."

As the missionary told the story, Dave and Becky both

remembered the night they heard the strange sounds outside their camper. Dave looked at Becky, then turned back to the missionary. "That's exactly how it happened!" The man's story fit exactly with their experience on the other side of that truck camper window, except that neither of them suspected that the sound they heard came from a gun that had twice been pointed at Dave's head, only to misfire each time.

DELIVER US FROM EVIL

When Jesus taught His followers to pray, He told them to say, "Deliver us from evil." It is, in all its simplicity, a threefold acknowledgment.

"Deliver us from evil" acknowledges the existence of evil. Jesus doesn't pretend that evil is a mere state of mind or a lie we must "rise above," as one songwriter sardonically says. On the contrary, Jesus tells us that we live in a fallen world—a world in which people try to kill one another. A world where a woman's womb is often a dangerous place to be—especially for females. A world where people shoot down passenger planes, where masked militants behead journalists and aid workers, where young girls are kidnapped from school and given as wives to terrorists. A world in which people steal from others, lie to others, hurt others.

"Deliver us from evil" acknowledges that we need deliverance. We don't need to deny the evil that surrounds and threatens (and sometimes overwhelms) us. We don't need to detach ourselves from the real world where evil seems all too prevalent. We need deliverance from it. We need to avoid it and escape it. We need to be shielded from it or through it. We need something like David's stones to defeat evil or the presence

that protected the three Hebrews and enabled them to emerge unharmed from the fiery furnace.

"Deliver us from evil" acknowledges that we can be delivered. When Jesus included the phrase "Deliver us from evil" in His model prayer, He clearly wanted His followers to understand that deliverance was possible. Philip Keller wrote:

> *Our Master was not one to engage in double-talk. He did not say one thing and mean another. He would not teach us to ask our heavenly Father for deliverance from evil if no deliverance was available. He would not instruct us to pray to be delivered from evil situations if our Father was unable to do so. But He is. And therein lies a great measure of the glory and joy of really knowing God as our Father.[1]*

According to Jesus, evil exists. It assails us. It threatens us. We need deliverance, and deliverance is possible. It is obtainable. It is available. "Pray then like this," Jesus said: "Deliver us from evil."

PRAY, "DELIVER US FROM DOING EVIL"

Our first instinct when praying the Lord's Prayer and saying, "Deliver us from evil," is to envision the evil that exists all around us—drunk drivers, corrupt officials, angry mobs. But as Aleksandr Solzhenitsyn famously pointed out, evil often lives much closer to home:

> *If only it were all so simple! If only there were evil people somewhere insidiously committing evil deeds, and it*

were necessary only to separate them from the rest of us and destroy them. But the line dividing good and evil cuts through the heart of every human being.[2]

To pray only for deliverance from the evil around us ignores that which is often the most destructive and debilitating evil—not the evil of bloodthirsty despots, deranged killers, or tyrannical bosses but the darkness and corruption of our own hearts. The most dangerous evil most of us face is that which hides inside. Paul, the great church planter of the first century, wrote:

> *I do not understand my own actions. For I do not do what I want, but I do the very thing I hate.* . . . *For I know that nothing good dwells in me, that is, in my flesh. For I have the desire to do what is right, but not the ability to carry it out. For I do not do the good I want, but the evil I do not want is what I keep on doing.* . . .
> *So I find it to be a law that when I want to do right, evil lies close at hand. For I delight in the law of God, in my inner being, but I see in my members another law waging war against the law of my mind and making me captive to the law of sin that dwells in my members. Wretched man that I am! Who will deliver me from this body of death? Thanks be to God through Jesus Christ our Lord!*[3]

So when you pray, "Deliver us from evil," pray for deliverance from *doing* evil. Pray for deliverance from the evil that "lies close at hand."[4] Pray for the righteousness of Christ to triumph over the wretchedness of your all-too-human heart. Pray for "Thanks be to God" to resound "through Jesus Christ our Lord" in your thoughts, words, and deeds.

PRAY, "DELIVER US FROM EVIL DONE TO US"

I was once a young man, believe it or not.

My wife and I had been married less than a year. I had been attending college in Findlay, Ohio, and working the eleven-to-seven shift at 7-11 in nearby Fostoria, Ohio. Yes, that's right. I was working 11–7 at 7-11. It would have been particularly poetic if I had still been working there on July 11.

But in early June that year, I gave my notice to my boss at 7-11, and a week or two later, my wife and I packed our few possessions and headed off to a summer job preparatory to beginning an intense course of ministry training in the fall.

The night after my final shift, the Fostoria 7-11 was robbed. For the first time. At gunpoint. During the 11–7 shift.

No one was hurt. But I was nonetheless relieved and grateful when I heard the news. I felt like a "brand plucked from the fire."[5] I had been delivered from evil.

That's very likely the idea Jesus had in mind when He included the phrase "Deliver us from evil" in His signature prayer. Jewish prayers both before and after Jesus' time often included similar petitions. Rabbi Judah ben Tema is said to have prayed:

Let it be thy good pleasure to deliver us from impudent men, and from impudence: from an evil man and an evil chance; from an evil affection, an evil companion,

and an evil neighbor: from Satan the destroyer, from a
hard judgment, and a hard adversary.[6]

That's the idea. Pray to be delivered from evil. From armed robbery. From debt and bankruptcy. From crop failure. From drivers who text while driving. From liars, gossips, and thieves. From evil affections, evil companions, and evil neighbors. From medical malpractice. From unscrupulous lawyers and corrupt judges. From bad bosses and bad employees. From addictions and obsessions. From every trick and technique of your enemy, the devil,[7] who "prowls around like a roaring lion, seeking someone to devour."[8]

Pray, "Deliver Us from the Evil Surrounding Us"

Every day we face numerous dangers, big and small, from the hazards of our drive to work to the thunderstorm that rolls through while we sleep. But we are not alone. We are surrounded by people facing similar threats—and many larger, more urgent ones as well.

That's why it is important to notice that the final petition Jesus gave His followers in what we call the Lord's Prayer contains the plural pronoun *us.* Just as we pray to "*Our* Father" to "give *us*" and "forgive *us*" and "lead *us*," so we pray, "Deliver *us.*" It is a corporate prayer. It is a prayer I must pray not only for myself but also for others.

You and I are surrounded by evil, and we are surrounded by people who need deliverance from those evils: My friend who teaches in the inner city and faces danger and discouragement on a daily basis. My many pastor friends, who bear heavy burdens and try to meet great demands while also maintaining healthy marriages and families. My friend who just lost his job. My servicemen nephews in Iraq and Afghanistan. My undercover police officer friend who faces extreme danger night after night. My grandchildren, who wrestle with cystic fibrosis and its implications day in and day out. My friend who contends with fibromyalgia. My friends who are healing from divorce. My friend who continues to courageously and graciously battle renal cancer. My paraplegic friend who is adjusting to life without her husband, who died last August.

Those people come to mind when I pray, "Deliver us from evil." So do many people I *don't* know. People I hear about in the news. People affected by crime or corruption. People hurt or made homeless by earthquakes, tornadoes, or hurricanes. People left jobless when a local business closes. People who pass me in ambulances or police cars.

Yesterday, while others in my family enjoyed a Sunday afternoon nap, I sat in a chair on our back deck, reading a book by one of my favorite authors. My four-year-old granddaughter tiptoed through the back door and asked me what I was doing.

"I'm just reading and enjoying this beautiful day."

"Me too." She carried a backpack with crayons and paper in it and parked herself at the table nearby.

Soon we heard sirens. We live in a quiet suburban neighborhood, so we don't hear as many sirens as some people do.

"What's that?" she asked.

I explained that it was a siren, probably on a police car or an ambulance.

Her expression turned somber. "Someone's in trouble."

I nodded. "Maybe we should pray."

"You pray."

So I did. I started my prayer, "Deliver us from evil," and went on briefly (she's only four, remember) to ask God to help whoever was in trouble.

I know it's a long shot, but I hope she remembers that. I hope sirens become an occasion for prayer to her. I hope the same for you. I hope you'll pray, "Deliver us from evil," often, on all sorts of occasions, for all sorts of people, against the evil that surrounds us.

Robert Benson wrote:

> *If we pray, and if we believe that God listens to our prayer, then to spend that audience on behalf of someone else is an act of selflessness that is larger than it seems. At some level, our prayer—spoken or unspoken, written or read aloud, experienced in silence or lived out in the work of our hands and feet—is all that we have to offer each other. And it can be the best that we ever give each other as well.[9]*

It is a simple prayer but one that is also rich in purpose and power. It is part of the Christ-follower's arsenal, detailed in Ephesians 6, where we are told to pray "at all times in the Spirit, with all prayer and supplication...with all perseverance, making supplication for all the saints."[10]

Pray it. Pray it daily. Pray it fervently. Pray it "at all times." Pray it for yourself and for others. Pray it for those around you. Pray it for your spouse and children. Pray it for your pastors and your church. Pray it for your neighborhood, city, state, nation, and world.

Finally, pray it in faith. Pray, "Deliver us from evil," believing that Jesus would not have taught His followers to pray it if it were not a prayer that would be answered.

Saint Cyprian, bishop of Carthage in the third century, wrote:

> *When we say, "Deliver us from evil," there remains nothing further which ought to be asked. When we have once asked for God's protection against evil and have obtained it, then we stand secure and safe against everything which the Devil and the world work against us.*[11]

> *Lord God Almighty, deliver us from evil.*
> *King of heaven, deliver us from evil.*
> *Ruler of all, deliver us from evil.*
> *Deliver us from doing evil, from the evil that "lies close at hand."*[12] *Let the righteousness of Christ triumph over the wretchedness of our all-too-human hearts.*
> *Deliver us from evil men and women, from evil affections, companions, and neighbors. Deliver us from dangers near and far, from liars, gossips, and thieves. From malpractice and injustice. From bad bosses and bad employees. From addictions and obsessions. Deliver us from every trick and technique of our enemy, the devil,*[13] *who "prowls around like a roaring lion, seeking someone to devour."*[14]
> *Deliver also those around us who need deliverance from evil. Deliver our suffering family and friends. Deliver those affected by crime or corruption, those who have been hurt or made homeless by earthquakes,*

tornadoes, or hurricanes. Deliver from joblessness, poverty, hunger, and disease.

Deliver us from evil, in Jesus' name, amen.

14

PRAY WORSHIPFULLY

—

My wife laughs at me.

She does it a lot but maybe most predictably at baseball games. I'm a lifelong Cincinnati Reds fan, and we recently attended a game at Great American Ballpark, the Reds' home field. We climbed to the very top row of seats as our tickets indicated and sat at the top corner of the section next to the "gap," a break in the structure providing an unobstructed view up Walnut Street from the ballpark.

Even there, I couldn't help myself. You see, I talk throughout the game. To the players. The umpires. Even sometimes to the ball itself.

"I don't know, Blue, looked like a ball from here."

"Come on, Billy, you've got him where you want him."

"Nice play, BP, way to go!"

"Get outta here!"

You get the idea. I know, of course, that they can't hear me. But I can't help myself. It's how I watch the game. It's how I root for my team.

Why? I'm not sure. I'm not even sure why I place so much importance on my favorite team's performance. Why do their wins make me happy? Why do their losses make me sad? Why do I even get angry when they make mistakes? And why do I feel proud when they make the playoffs?

They're my hometown team, sure. But what does that mean? As Jerry Seinfeld once said, "Loyalty to any one sports team is pretty hard to justify. Because the players are always changing, the team can move to another city. You're actually rooting for the clothes, when you get right down to it. You know what I mean? You are standing and cheering and yelling for your clothes to beat the clothes from another city."[1]

He has a point. We cheer for a group of athletes we had no part in choosing or assembling, some of whom played for a different team last year—or will play for a new team next year. We have contributed nothing to their failure or success. We don't know them personally. We do not pay them. We have not coached them. They simply play for a school we attend or a city we live in (or near)—or where we *once* attended or lived, even if it was decades ago.

Yet we exult when they do well and get upset when they do poorly. We brag about their wins and tease others whose teams lose. We expend great effort in attending or watching games, reading stats and standings, and celebrating or grieving according to their progress. We even buy and wear shirts with their logos and the number of our favorite player.

What's that all about? Why do we invest such effort and emotion into sports teams and their performance? I think it has something to do with the universal human need to worship, to identify with someone or something greater than ourselves. We feel happier—more complete—when we feel connected to something great, something glorious, something powerful and wonderful and worthy of applause, loyalty, and honor.

In his landmark book, *The Purpose-Driven Life*, Rick Warren wrote:

> *Anthropologists have noted that worship is a universal urge, hard-wired by God into the very fiber of our*

*being—an inbuilt need to connect with God. Worship
is as natural as eating or breathing. If we fail to worship
God, we always find a substitute, even if it ends up
being ourselves.*[2]

Everyone, everywhere, in all nations, from all races, instinctively feels this. From the beginning of time, human beings have felt the need to worship. Every civilization in the history of the human race has felt and recognized and exhibited this need.

Whether it was the Babylonians worshipping the stars, the Greeks worshipping the pantheon of gods on Mount Olympus, the Egyptians worshipping Ra, or the Native Americans worshipping the sun god, men and women feel an innate need to worship something or someone higher than themselves.

For instance, did you know that there is a church of Kennedy worshippers? I kid you not: a group that believes that worshipping the late President John F. Kennedy can cure them of congenital, even terminal diseases.

There is also the Ministry of Universal Wisdom, a church based on a belief in flying saucers. There is a Wiccan group, one of many, called the New Reformed Orthodox Order of the Golden Dawn. There is an Astrological, Metaphysical, Occult, Revelatory, Enlightenment Church! I'm not sure if they call themselves AMORE Church for short.

And I could go on: the Etherian Religious Society of Universal Brotherhood, the Aquarian Fellowship Church, and the Reformed Druids of North America (because who wants to be an unreformed Druid?).

There are drug-oriented churches like the Church of the Awakening. Uh-huh. And mail-order churches like the Brotherhood of Peace and Tranquility. And Internet churches like the International Christian Internet Church. The Universal Christian International Catholic Church (if it's universal, isn't it redundant to call it "international"?). The American Carpatho-Russian Orthodox Greek Catholic Church (huh?). The Latter House of the Lord for All People and the Church of the Mountain, Apostolic Faith (that's quite a mouthful).

There is even a Church of Spiritual Humanism, a Church of the Humanitarian God, and the United Secularists of America. Because even atheists and humanists feel the need to worship; they typically worship human effort and achievement, while secularists and rationalists tend to worship science and reason. Naturalists tend to deify nature. Socialists and communists typically exalt the state. Narcissists have the most pathetic god of all: they worship themselves (you'll find a lot of that in the entertainment industry. . .and publishing. Present company excepted, of course).

It is a universal human need. We are drawn upward. We long to experience the supernatural, to respond to the transcendent, to praise that which is bigger and better and greater than us.

WORSHIP ROCKS

Prayer connects us to the transcendent God. When Jesus taught His followers to pray, He told them to enter prayer as children addressing a tender, loving father: "Our Father." But with His next words He also told them to acknowledge the glory, kingdom, and power of God. He instructed His *talmidim* to identify and align themselves with God's reputation, God's rule, and God's will. Doing so not only meets our deeply felt human need but also positions us to pray effectively and powerfully.

It's no wonder, then, that Christians from the earliest days until now have added a biblical doxology to the Lord's Prayer: "For thine is the kingdom, and the power, and the glory, for ever. Amen."[3] The words echo the first lines of King David's prayer of praise upon receiving the gifts of God's people for the building of the temple in Jerusalem:

> *"Yours, O LORD, is the greatness,*
> *The power and the glory,*
> *The victory and the majesty;*
> *For all that is in heaven and in earth is Yours;*
> *Yours is the kingdom, O LORD,*
> *And You are exalted as head over all."*[4]

How wonderful and fitting that King David's doxology has long been appended to the Son of David's prayer! Theologian N. T. Wright explains:

> *This concluding doxology doesn't appear in the best*
> *manuscripts of either Matthew or Luke, and it is*
> *only comparatively recently, in the last few centuries,*
> *that it has been restored to the liturgy of the Western*
> *church. But it was already well established within*
> *a century or so of Jesus' day; and it is actually*
> *inconceivable, within the Jewish praying styles*
> *of his day, that Jesus would have intended the*

prayer to stop simply with 'deliver us from evil'.
Something like this must have been intended from
the beginning. In any case, it chimes in exactly
with the message of the prayer as a whole: God's
kingdom, God's power, and God's glory are what it's
all about. [5]

The message of the Lord's Prayer as a whole echoes the tone of all Jesus taught and modeled about prayer. According to Jesus, praise is not just one way (among many) to pray; it must be the tone of prayer from beginning ("May your Name be kept holy. May your Kingdom come, your will be done on earth as in heaven" [6]) to end ("For kingship, power and glory are yours forever" [7]).

In fact, the final phrase of the Lord's Prayer (which was in use at least from the end of the first century, as revealed in the *Didache*, a church manual probably composed just a few decades after Jesus' lifetime) clearly mirrors the first three petitions, albeit in slightly different order:

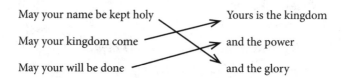

May your name be kept holy   Yours is the kingdom

May your kingdom come   and the power

May your will be done   and the glory

The difference seems perfectly understandable. As we begin to pray the Lord's Prayer, our first three petitions proceed from the most abstract and universal to the more specific and personal. We pray for His glory—His reputation, the glory of His name throughout the universe—and then for

His kingdom to come on this earth, and finally for His will to be done not only outside of us but in us as well. Then, having prayed for bread and grace and leadership and deliverance in the rest of the Lord's Prayer, it seems logical to praise God for His kingship (authority), through which He exercises His power (ability), thus bringing about His glory (acclaim).

These are more than mere phrases. Each phrase in this doxology helps those who pray it to respond to the transcendent and praise the One who is bigger and better and greater than us, thus meeting our needs, focusing our minds, and changing our lives.

PRAY, "YOURS IS THE KINGDOM; I BOW"

When you pray, "Yours is the kingdom," you are acknowledging and welcoming the rule of God in the world around you and the world inside you.

More than three hundred years before Jesus' lifetime, Alexander the Great strode through the civilized world, conquering and subduing everything in his path. In 332 BC, after humiliating the mighty Persian Empire of Darius III and conquering Persia's naval bases along the Mediterranean coastline, Alexander marched south to Egypt. He was welcomed by Mazaces, who had been the Persian governor of Egypt, who handed over Egypt's treasury and palaces to the new emperor. Alexander installed a garrison at the eastern city of Pelusium and sailed south on the Nile. The victorious conqueror and his troops sailed past gleaming pyramids and obelisks and finally reached Memphis, the ancient capital city, where he was rapturously hailed as a liberator—a savior from the hated Persians—and acclaimed as the new "master of the universe." He was crowned as pharaoh and anointed as "son of the gods" in Memphis on November 14, 332 BC.

The knowledge of those events may have made the phrase "Yours is the kingdom" richer and weightier to Jesus' first followers than it may be to us. But that sort of scene should occupy our minds when we pray, "Yours is the kingdom." It welcomes our King as Savior and Liberator and crowns Him in our hearts and lives as Master and Lord. It looks back to the announcement of John the Baptist in the wilderness by the Jordan ("Repent, for the kingdom of heaven is at hand"[8]) and looks forward to that moment in the future when the seventh angel will blow on a shofar and the inhabitants of heaven will shout, "The kingdom of the world has become the kingdom of our Lord and of his Christ, and he shall reign forever and ever."[9]

Just as we align ourselves with the reputation, rule, and will of God when we begin to pray, we must also view all our petitions, prayers, intercessions, and thanksgivings in light of the fact that God is King! Therefore, "Yours is the kingdom" informs our request for daily bread (our King can open the treasury to us). "Yours is the kingdom" influences our appeal for forgiveness (our King has every right and intention to grant pardons). "Yours is the kingdom" instructs our plea for Him to lead us (the King Himself is on the throne; He will not fail to lead us). And "yours is the kingdom" encourages us to expect deliverance from evil (it is the King's pleasure to protect His subjects).

So pray, "Yours is the kingdom; I bow." Picture yourself in His throne room. See Him high and lifted up. Envision His smile and His scepter extended in your direction. Bow to the

King. Bend your knee. Throw yourself at His feet.

Then remember that He is your Father, your Abba, your Daddy. The King on the throne, like the father in Jesus' story of the prodigal son, will run to meet you as you stumble toward Him. He will lift you up and kiss your face. He will tousle your hair and hug you tight. And because the kingdom is His, you have no reason to doubt that He will grant all your requests.

PRAY, "YOURS IS THE POWER; I OBEY"

When Jesus walked the earth, He met many people. Lepers. Prostitutes. Pharisees. Priests. Samaritans. Fishermen. Tax collectors. Governors. But of all the people He met, we know of only one who impressed Him.

Had you been there at the time, you wouldn't have expected Jesus to be impressed with this guy. Oh, he was important to many. He was a soldier—a Roman centurion, in fact. But he was very likely not the first centurion Jesus ever met. Roman soldiers were everywhere He went, and therefore centurions—who commanded a hundred soldiers—were everywhere as well. Most importantly, though, this man was not Jewish, and Jesus, as a rabbi, focused mostly on Jews.

Yet the man came to Him one day when Jesus had just arrived home from a teaching tour in the area. The centurion strode toward the Rabbi and stood in front of Him.

"Lord," he said. Well, that was a surprise right there. It was not a theological statement but a term of respect, much like our word *sir*. The guy with the sword called the guy with no sword "Lord."

He went on. "My servant is lying paralyzed at home, suffering terribly."

Jesus may have scrutinized the man's face. He may have pondered his schedule. Or He may have answered quickly. "I will come and heal him."

The centurion held up a hand. "Lord," he said again. "I am not worthy to have you come under my roof, but only say the word, and my servant will be healed." Jesus may have blinked because the centurion felt the need to explain. "I too am a man under authority, with soldiers under me. And I say to one, 'Go,' and he goes, and to another, 'Come,' and he comes, and to my servant, 'Do this,' and he does it." In other words, he fully believed that Jesus had the power and authority to command whatever or whoever was afflicting his servant to leave him alone.

That is when both Gospel writers who recorded this event say Jesus "marveled."

Jesus turned and spoke to the followers and onlookers who dogged His steps everywhere He went. "I tell you, with no one in Israel have I found such faith." Then He turned back to the centurion and nodded. "Go; let it be done for you as you have believed."[10]

Both Matthew and Luke report that the centurion's servant was healed at that very moment, just as the centurion believed.

When you pray, "Yours is the power," you are coming as the centurion came. You are saying, "You can heal, if You just say the word." You are saying, "You can provide, if You just say the word." You are saying, "You can forgive, lead, deliver—if You just say the word." You are saying, "You can do anything, if You just say the word. Nothing is too difficult for You."

To pray, "Yours is the power," is to say not only, "You can," but "I will." It is the echo of "Your will be done, on earth as it is in heaven."[11] It is the punctuation of that sentence. It is not only a recognition of God's power but a submission to it. By saying, "Yours is the power," we say, "Not ours." "Yours is the power" means "Not mine."

We often pray as though the power is—or should be—ours. We want God to agree to our wishes. We want Him to sign up for our agenda. But "Yours is the power" signs us up for *His* agenda. We present our requests and then say—like the centurion—"Only say the word." We let our desires be known and then leave them with the One who has the power and authority to command.

So when you pray, "Yours is the power," say it like the centurion saying, "Only say the word."[12] Pray, "Not my will, but yours, be done."[13] Pray, "Not as I will, but as you will."[14] Pray, "I delight to do your will, O my God."[15] Pray, "Yours is the power; I obey."

PRAY, "YOURS IS THE GLORY; I WORSHIP"

When we pray, "Yours is the kingdom, the power, and the glory," we are not making a request; we are stating a fact. We are not asking for God to have the kingdom, power, and glory, but we are saying those things are His already. Our prayers simply acknowledge that fact.

It is no mistake that the phrase is introduced with the word *for*. That word connects "Yours is the kingdom, the power, and the glory" with all that went before. So one way to understand the phrase in its fullness is to chart it like this:

Our Father in heaven. . .
for Yours is the kingdom, the power, and the glory
May Your name be kept holy. . .
for Yours is the kingdom, the power, and the glory
May Your kingdom come. . .
for Yours is the kingdom, the power, and the glory
May Your will be done. . .
for Yours is the kingdom, the power, and the glory
Give us this day our daily bread. . .
for Yours is the kingdom, the power, and the glory
Forgive us our sins. . .
for Yours is the kingdom, the power, and the glory
As we forgive others. . .
for Yours is the kingdom, the power, and the glory
And lead us. . .not into temptation. . .
for Yours is the kingdom, the power, and the glory
Deliver us from evil. . .
for yours is the kingdom, the power, and the glory.

Looking at the Lord's Prayer that way helps me to see how every affirmation and petition relates to the kingship, will, and glory of God. It helps me especially to see how each of these things reflects God's glory.

If I pray communally, in unity with Jesus, the Spirit, and the Church. . .that will surely bring glory to God.

If I pray cooperatively—aligning myself with God's reputation, kingdom, and will in everything I ask and do— that will bring glory to God.

If I trust Him to provide my needs—and He does—the glory is His!

If I walk in forgiveness and holiness—the glory is His!

If I relay that same grace to others, forgiving them as I've been forgiven—the glory is His!

If I let Him lead me, day by day, step by step—the glory is His!

If I experience deliverance from evil—the glory is His!

Because the kingdom is His, the power is His. And because the kingdom and power are His, all the glory is His.

So pray, "Yours is the glory. . .I worship." Pour out your love, your hopes, dreams, needs, and wants to God, expressing them all to Him in submission, obedience, and worship.

Yours, O Lord, is the greatness,
the power and the glory,
the victory and the majesty;
for all that is in heaven and in earth is Yours;
Yours is the kingdom, O Lord,
and You are exalted as head over all.[16]
Help me to live a life that says,
"Yours is the kingdom; I bow,"
"Yours is the power; I obey," and
"Yours is the glory; I worship."
In Jesus' name, amen.

15

Pray Gratefully

⁓

I was at my wit's end.

I was a pastor of a wonderful church. A lovely wife, loving family, and caring friends surrounded me. I enjoyed good health. Yet for the first time in my life, I was depressed. Not just down. Not just discouraged. Depressed.

It had been coming for months, and it was to last for months to come, though eventually I did climb out of that strange, dark place. But I didn't do it alone. My deliverance was a gift of God and an answer to prayer, just to be clear. But weekly sessions with a good counselor also helped. So did some overdue changes in diet and exercise, as well as an adrenal fatigue supplement and a low daily dose of an antidepressant. I'm convinced the biggest contributor to my recovery, however, was prayer.

Sure, sure, sure. You would expect a pastor to say that, I know. But seriously. God is my salvation from depression, and prayer was a daily means of grace to me. Some days my praying was fairly unintelligible and often repetitive (along the lines of "Lord, have mercy; Christ, have mercy; Lord, have mercy, have mercy, have mercy"—that kind of thing). But as I look back in my prayer journal over the two years or so of my depression, I can see how prayer sustained me (one of many terrific reasons, by the way, to keep a prayer journal). But even more important than all my cries for help and relief and deliverance were my nightly prayers of thanks.

I honestly can't recall if my counselor suggested it or if I came up with the idea. It was probably me; let's go with that. But at some point in my battle with depression, I determined never to lay my head on my pillow for the night without recording in my journal at least three prayers of thanks.

Sometimes I gave thanks for simple things:

Abba, thank You for the hummingbird I watched just moments ago, and for the sparrow that nearly lit on my lap. Thank You for the beauty and functionality of Your creation.

Sometimes (just across the page from that last prayer) I gave thanks on special occasions:

Abba, THANK YOU! for my wife of thirty-one years, and this day on which we celebrate our anniversary. Thank You for all You've given me through her, all You've taught me through her, all the ways You've changed me through her, and all the blessings that are mine because of her, chief among them being, of course, herself.

And some were for fairly ordinary blessings:

Thank You, Lord, for all your kindness to me: for a day of health and work and time with family. Thank You that I so often get to see my children and grandchildren. Thank You that I get to sleep in comfort tonight and preach Your Word tomorrow.

Day by day, however, by giving thanks for just three things—and many days, of course, I exceeded the minimum I had set for myself—I found my focus shifting from all the things that seemed to be wrong in my life to the many more things that were right and good and even wonderful.

I want to be careful not to minimize the reality and seriousness of depression. It can be debilitating and even life-threatening, and I'm not suggesting that "cheer up" is a meaningful prescription for overcoming it. Remember, my recovery included counseling, medication, diet, exercise, and more. But I believe nonetheless that praying gratefully was tremendously influential in overcoming my depression.

I think that is part of the reason Jesus clearly modeled this kind of praying. Praying gratefully is both vaccine and antidote to depression, discouragement, bitterness, and resentment. "Giving thanks," wrote E. M. Bounds, "is the very life of prayer. It is its fragrance and music, its poetry and its crown."[1]

SAY THANK YOU

My two-and-a-half-year-old grandson Ryder hasn't yet caught on. He is still learning the basics of good manners. So I love to remind him when he receives something—a popsicle, help putting on his shoes, a cup of water: "Say thank you, Ryder."

And he will invariably respond, "Thank you, Ryder."

He doesn't get it, of course, but I do. And isn't that what really matters?

It is among the first lessons of childhood: "What do you say?" The correct answer, of course, is thank you (unless the situation calls for "please" or "excuse me").

You may not remember, but you probably had to be taught to say thank you, too. Maybe you still do. Maybe, like me, you could use an occasional reminder like the ones we used to get from our parents: "What do you say?"

The Gospel writers tell us in several places that Jesus often went off somewhere to pray. But there are just a few occasions when they actually recorded Jesus praying. One of those is in John 11, which relates the raising of Lazarus from the dead. John, who was there that day, tells us:

> Then Jesus, deeply moved again, came to the tomb. It was a cave, and a stone lay against it. Jesus said, "Take away the stone." Martha, the sister of the dead man, said to him, "Lord, by this time there will be an odor, for he has been dead four days." Jesus said to her, "Did I not tell you that if you believed you would see the glory of God?" So they took away the stone. And Jesus lifted up his eyes and said, "Father, I thank you that you have heard me. I knew that you always hear me, but I said this on account of the people standing around, that they may believe that you sent me." When he had said these things, he cried out with a loud voice, "Lazarus, come out." The man who had died came out, his hands and feet bound with linen strips, and his face wrapped with a cloth. Jesus said to them, "Unbind him, and let him go." [2]

Jesus looked up over the heads of the crowd—probably skyward—and said thank you. And it's fascinating that we can't be sure what he thanked the Father for. He said, "I thank You that You have heard me." Was that a thank you for a prayer

He had already prayed? For something He was praying as He talked to Martha? Did He receive some subtle assurance that the Father had been listening? Was He thanking the Father in advance for the resurrection of Lazarus? We don't know. Scholars differ.

But we do know a few important things.

1. Jesus said thank you. Let that sink in for a minute. Jesus—by whom, through whom, and for whom "all things were created, in heaven and on earth, visible and invisible, whether thrones or dominions or rulers or authorities."[3] *That* guy said thank you. The One who commands legions of angels. The One who calms the seas and raises the dead. The Son of God. He said, "Thank You for hearing me." If anyone could have taken it for granted that His prayers would be heard—that all of heaven itself would hang on His every word—it would have been Jesus. But He took no such thing for granted. He said thank you.

2. He said it aloud for the benefit of others. He could have said a silent prayer of thanks. But He lifted his eyes and said thank you aloud. He even went on to specify that He did it that way for the benefit of others. Like a parent who thanks the cashier at the grocery store or the crossing guard on the way to school while his or her child watches, Jesus thanked the Father visibly and verbally so that others—including you and me, perhaps—might learn from His example.

3. He said it aloud so others may believe that the Father sent Him. The Son's grateful prayer to the Father—especially coming, as it did, right before the raising of Lazarus from the dead—helped to establish His bona fides. The prayer was a witness to the person and mission of Jesus Christ.

It is much the same when *you* pray gratefully. Your thank-yous to the Father turn your eyes heavenward. They act as a vaccine and antidote to depression, discouragement, bitterness, and resentment. They set an example to others who might hear. They witness to the presence and influence of God in your life.

So, "What do you say?"

Say thank you. Say it sincerely. Say it often. Say it habitually. Maybe journal your thank-yous, as I still do to this day. Maybe tweet or text them. Maybe say thank you each night as you lay your head on your pillow. Maybe say it as your feet hit the floor the next morning (though that may be a stretch if you're as far from a morning person as I am). But say it: thank you. It's one of the simplest—and best—prayers you can pray.

SAY, "THANK YOU ANYWAY"

It had been a tough week for Jesus. Maybe a tough month. Or more.

His cousin, John the Baptist, had been arrested and tossed into a filthy dungeon. Things were looking bleak for the camel-hair-wearing prophet. So he sent a couple of his disciples to Jesus with a message: "Are you the Messiah we've been expecting, or should we keep looking for someone else?" [4]

Ouch. His own cousin, who had announced him as the Lamb of God, apparently didn't like the way things were going. He was having doubts. That seemed to set Jesus off, as Matthew tells the story. Jesus sent a message back to John and praised his cousin, saying, "Of all who have ever lived, none is greater than John the Baptist." [5] But then He went on to point out how fickle and childish people were and "began to denounce the cities where most of his mighty works had been done."[6]

Then the strangest thing happened. Of all times for Jesus to give thanks, He chose that moment. Immediately following His denunciation of that fickle generation and those unrepentant cities, Matthew reports:

> *At that time Jesus declared, "I thank you, Father, Lord of heaven and earth, that you have hidden these things from the wise and understanding and revealed them to little children; yes, Father, for such was your gracious will."[7]*

Huh? Your cousin is having a crisis of faith—in You? And You're in the midst of a fickle bunch of people? And the cities where You've done a whole bunch of miracles seem unimpressed? And You say, "Thank You, Father"?

Exactly right. What a great time to give thanks. Even in the midst of discouraging circumstances, Jesus prayed gratefully. He looked for—and saw—the Father at work, even though things appeared to be going not so well.

What an example. Jesus shows us how to pray, "Thank You anyway."

So—having a tough week. . .or month? Say, "Thank You anyway."

Your car broke down? In traffic? On the bridge? Say, "Thank You anyway."

Had to miss work because you couldn't afford to put gas in your car? Say, "Thank You anyway."

Got a speeding ticket on your way to pay your last speeding ticket? Say, "Thank You anyway."

Got the hiccups right before your choir audition? Say, "Thank You anyway."

Absentmindedly took a sleeping pill and a laxative at the same time? Say, "Thank You anyway."

The Bible says, "Give thanks in all circumstances; for this is the will of God in Christ Jesus for you."[8] *The Message* paraphrase puts it like this: "Thank God no matter what happens. This is the way God wants you who belong to Christ Jesus to live."[9] It may sound ridiculous, even impossible, but saying, "Thank You anyway," is a great habit to cultivate for several reasons.

1. It opens your eyes. When I'm going through tough times and I start thanking God in the midst of those tough times, it's amazing how quickly my mind clears and my eyes are opened to the multitude of things in my life that *aren't* going wrong. Sometimes I even see God's hand in the things that are happening—as Jesus did when He said, "Thank you. . .that you have hidden these things from the wise and understanding and revealed them to little children"—and what before had looked like just an unredeemable mess became an opportunity for grace or witness or even laughter. At my lowest point in my bout with depression, the only time in my life I've ever been so low as to spend a whole day in bed, I journaled this prayer the next day: "Thank You, Lord, for the suffering of recent weeks and for what You are teaching me and accomplishing in me through it! Thank You for teaching me about suffering and leadership and faithfulness and steadfastness. Thank You for reminding me that when I am weak, You are strong."

2. It lifts your spirits. Saying, "Thank You anyway," often has a snowball effect. You may say it grudgingly at first. But it's hard to say thank you for very long without feeling your spirits lift, your strength return, and—sometimes—seeing your situation improve. Try it. Imitate Jesus. Say something like, "Thank You, Father, Lord of heaven and earth, that even though I have a flat tire on this busy road, I have a spare in the trunk." Or "Thank You, Father, Lord of heaven and earth, that even though I have a flat tire on this busy road, I have a car." Or even "Thank You, Father, Lord of heaven and earth, that even though I have a flat tire on this busy road, and am going to be late for my appointment, I may yet meet a tow truck driver or a Good Samaritan who represents an appointment You've made for me." That kind of praying can turn a threatening storm cloud into showers of blessing.

3. It glorifies God. Just as my grandchildren watch me say thank you to a store clerk or a restaurant server, people are watching you. And when they see or hear you say, "Thank You anyway," they may "see your good deeds and glorify your Father in heaven."[10] They may someday ask why things don't affect you the same way they seem to affect other people. Their eyes or hearts may be opened to the God who gives you the command—and the strength—to "Thank God no matter what happens."[11]

SAY THANK YOU ALWAYS

The Gospel writer Luke records Jesus' appearance to two of His followers on the road to Emmaus later in the day of His resurrection. Somewhere on that seven-mile journey, Jesus asked to walk with them, though they didn't recognize

Him. They agreed and talked with Jesus *about* Jesus and all the things that had everyone talking. . .and still they didn't recognize Jesus. When they reached their home in Emmaus, they invited their companion in. . .and still didn't know it was Jesus.

I'm not sure about the details of how that happened, but I find it fascinating when they finally did recognize Him:

> *When he was at table with them, he took the bread and*
> *blessed and broke it and gave it to them. And their eyes*
> *were opened, and they recognized him. And he vanished*
> *from their sight.*[12]

He took the bread and blessed it and broke it and gave it to them, Luke says. *That* is when their eyes were opened. Luke doesn't tell us whether it was the blessing of the bread, the breaking of it, or the offering of it—or all of the above— that opened their eyes. He doesn't say if there was something clearly characteristic of Jesus in the way He blessed the bread or broke it or offered it. He simply says that when He did that, they recognized Him.

Nothing could have been more common, more ordinary, for a first-century Jewish couple than for a Jewish companion to take the bread, bless it, break it, and share it. Even today, when an observant Jew takes a piece of bread in his hands, he will say, *"Baruch atah adonai elokeinu melech haolam hamotzie lechem myn ha'aretz"* (Blessed are You, Lord our God, King of the universe, who brings forth bread from the ground). It is a simple prayer of thanks. But for whatever reason, in whatever way, His grateful prayer revealed Jesus to them.

As Jesus said thank You in such a common way at such an ordinary time, so saying thank You always and everywhere will invite the presence of Jesus and transform the simplest meal into a resurrection appearance.

Anne Lamott, in her short book *Help Thanks Wow*, wrote:

> *Gratitude runs the gamut from shaking your head and saying, "Thanks, wow, I appreciate it so much," for your continued health, or a good day at work, or the first blooms of the daisies in the park, to saying, "Thanks, that's a relief," when it's not the transmission, or an abscess, or an audit notice from the IRS. "Thanks" can be the recognition that you have been blessed mildly, or with a feeling as intense as despair at the miracle of having been spared. You say Thankyouthankyouthankyouthankyou: My wife is going to live. We get to stay in this house. They found my son: he's in jail, but he's alive; we know where he is and he's safe for the night.*
>
> *Things could've gone either way, but they came down on our side. It could have been much worse, and it wasn't. Heads, we won.*
>
> *And of course, gratitude can be for everything in between.*[13]

Pray gratefully. Say thank You. Say, "Thank You anyway." Say thank You always. Say thank You for highs and lows alike. Say thank You for great deliverances and tiny graces and everything in between. Pray for the grace to pray this way, and give thanks for the ability to give thanks.

Gracious, giving Father, thank You.

Please give me the grace to pray gratefully.

Thank You for the ability—the breath, the mind, the tongue—to give thanks.

Teach me to say, "Thank You."

Teach me to say it every day, morning and evening.

Teach me to say, "Thank You anyway."

Remind me when storm clouds gather and I am tempted to curse or complain that Your Word tells me to "give thanks in all circumstances."[14]

Teach me to say thank You always—

for small favors and giant blessings,

for daily kindnesses and miraculous moments alike.

Save me, God, from ever taking You or any of Your gifts for granted.

In Jesus' name, amen.

16

PRAY BIBLICALLY

—

I thought I was through as a writer.

My energy was spent. My confidence was shot. My future looked bleak.

For most of the previous three years, I had tried and toiled through multiple drafts of a demanding book project. I had completed one revision after another. Some chapters had gone through more than two dozen distinct incarnations, and it had gotten to the point where I had lost objectivity. I was burned out, and I knew it.

I toughed it out, and eventually the project was finished and sent to the publisher. But I didn't know if I'd ever write anything again. I wasn't sure I even cared.

Then one day I got a call. An editor had seen a proposal I had sent months earlier, and while my proposal hadn't gone anywhere, she remembered it when she lost one of the writers for a new product called *The Prayer Bible*. She explained that the timeline was tight and asked if I would be interested. I told her—get this—that I'd pray about it.

I did and soon accepted the writing assignment.

I spent the next two months reading and praying through the latter half of the Old Testament, from Job through Malachi. As I prayed, I jotted down my prayers and added occasional notes and additional material.

I read Job's cry, "These are some of the minor things he does, merely a whisper of his power. Who can understand the thunder of his power?"[1] and prayed, "God of power and might, even the 'minor' things you do are amazing, though they merely whisper of your power. I praise you for all your works; they are much too wonderful for me to understand."[2]

I huddled in the cave of Adullum with David, and when he cried, "I am overwhelmed, and you alone know the way I should turn,"[3] I prayed, "Life overwhelms me, O God. You alone know the way I should go; please whisper your will in my ears with every step I take."[4]

When Ezekiel unfolded his vision of the valley of dry bones, I prayed, "Thank you, Father, for the regenerating power of the Holy Spirit. Empower me today to live in the newness of life that you have given me."[5]

As Daniel spent the night with lions, I prayed, "God, I thank you that you are able to keep me and protect me through every circumstance, and bring me into your 'glorious presence innocent of sin and with great joy' (Jude 24)."[6]

I prayed all the way through Malachi's prophecy, and after his fourth chapter, where he promised the coming Sun of Righteousness who would arise with "healing in his wings,"[7] I prayed, "Thank you, Father, for the healing righteousness that you sent through your Son, Jesus Christ. May he rise in more people's hearts, like the bright morning sun."[8]

By the time I sent those prayers, hymns, and marginal notes, my soul—and writing ministry—was revived. I was a new man. I had experienced anew the power of God's Word and the healing, renewing, restoring beauty of praying God's Word.

NOT BY BREAD ALONE

Many people know that Jesus, when He battled the evil one in the wilderness of Judea following His baptism, triumphed over the devil with scripture. When Satan tempted Him with hunger, Jesus quoted Deuteronomy 8:3: "Man does not live by bread alone, but man lives by every word that comes from the mouth of the LORD."[9] When tempted to stage an event that would reveal His glory, Jesus countered with Deuteronomy 6:16: "You shall not put the LORD your God to the test."[10] And when He was invited to bow down and worship Satan, Jesus dispatched His enemy with Deuteronomy 6:13, saying, "Away from me, Satan! For it is written: 'Worship the Lord your God, and serve him only.'"[11]

Jesus knew His Bible, of course. He used it to defeat temptation. But fewer people know that He also prayed scripture, leaving us an example to follow. How do we know this?

Remember the words of Jesus on the cross? Matthew and Mark both recorded Jesus' agonizing cry: "And about the ninth hour Jesus cried out with a loud voice, saying, 'Eli, Eli, lema sabachthani?' that is, 'My God, my God, why have you forsaken me?'"[12] From that moment to now, people have puzzled over His cry. Some at the scene thought He cried out to the prophet Elijah. Some today hear those words as an indication that Jesus felt forsaken in His last moments of life. Many theorize that the Father turned His face from Jesus, unable to look on Him because of all the sin He bore.

Amazingly, however, many miss the fact that Jesus' words were an apparent allusion to scripture, to the first line of the messianic Psalm 22. Other lines of that psalm, written hundreds of years earlier by King David, reflect—with startling accuracy—Jesus' situation on the cross:

> *I am. . .scorned by mankind and despised by the people.*
> *All who see me mock me;*
>> *they make mouths at me; they wag their heads;*
> *"He trusts in the LORD; let him deliver him;*
>> *let him rescue him, for he delights in him!". . .*

> *I am poured out like water,*
>> *and all my bones are out of joint;*
> *my heart is like wax;*
>> *it is melted within my breast;*
> *my strength is dried up like a potsherd,*
>> *and my tongue sticks to my jaws;*
>> *you lay me in the dust of death.*

> *For dogs encompass me;*
>> *a company of evildoers encircles me;*
> *they have pierced my hands and feet—*
> *I can count all my bones—*
> *they stare and gloat over me;*
> *they divide my garments among them,*
>> *and for my clothing they cast lots. . . .*

> *You who fear the LORD, praise him!*
>> *All you offspring of Jacob, glorify him,*
>> *and stand in awe of him, all you offspring of Israel!*
> *For he has not despised or abhorred*
>> *the affliction of the afflicted,*

> *and he has not hidden his face from him,*
> *but has heard, when he cried to him. . . .*
>
> *All the ends of the earth shall remember*
> *and turn to the* LORD,
> *and all the families of the nations*
> *shall worship before you.* [13]

Matthew and Mark tell us that Jesus spoke the first line of Psalm 22 "with a loud voice." Those words may have been all He had the strength to say; He may have lost consciousness after praying, "My God, my God, why have you forsaken me?" Or He may have gone on to pray the rest of the psalm weakly, even silently. Or He may have been employing the common technique rabbis used, a verbal shorthand in which part of a command or sentence served to evoke the whole, much as a modern speaker might say, "A penny saved," trusting others to mentally complete the proverb ("is a penny earned").

But there seems to be little doubt that Jesus, drawing from His Jewish upbringing and education, prayed biblically in that moment, drawing from the Davidic psalm that was most keenly applicable to His situation and most fully expressed His agony *and* His confident hope.

In fact, even with His last gasp, He prayed the words of scripture: "Then Jesus, calling out with a loud voice, said, 'Father, into your hands I commit my spirit!' And having said this he breathed his last."[14] With those words, the Son of David echoed the words of David from Psalm 31: "Into your hands I commit my spirit; deliver me, LORD, my faithful God."[15]

Don't miss the fact that Jesus could have prayed those two

Bible prayers silently. In fact, those two times Jesus prayed Scripture were the only times the Gospel writers described Jesus as speaking "with a loud voice"[16] from the cross. It was almost as if He wanted to be sure His followers heard those prayers. It is easy to imagine several reasons for that, and it wouldn't surprise me to learn that one reason was because there is great comfort, strength, and blessing in praying the Word of God.

PRAY THE PSALMS

I also don't think it is an accident that the two clear examples we have of Jesus praying scripture—in His moment of greatest agony and deepest need, no less—are both from the Psalms. Dr. Scot McKnight says, "Praying with Jesus means using the Psalms: His entire life was bathed with psalms."[17]

The Psalms have been the prayer book of God's people almost since they were first written. In fact, the second chapter of Jonah depicts the reluctant prophet—after he was thrown overboard and swallowed by a large fish—praying to God, and practically every line of his prayer is a quote from or allusion to a psalm:

"In my distress I called to the LORD,	*Psalm 8:6, 120:1*
and he answered me.	*Psalm 88:13*
From deep in the realm of the dead I called for help,	*Psalm 86:1–7*
and you listened to my cry.	
You hurled me into the depths,	
into the very heart of the seas,	
and the currents swirled about me;	*Psalm 69:1*

all your waves and breakers	*Psalm 42:7*
swept over me.	
I said, 'I have been banished	
from your sight;	*Psalm 31:22*
yet I will look again	
toward your holy temple.'	*Psalm 5:7*
The engulfing waters threatened me,	*Psalm 69:2*
the deep surrounded me;	*Psalm 18:5*
seaweed was wrapped around my head.	*Psalm 116:3*
To the roots of the mountains I sank down;	
the earth beneath barred me in forever.	
But you, LORD my God	*Psalm 30:3*
brought my life up from the pit.	
"When my life was ebbing away,	*Psalm 142:3*
I remembered you, LORD,	*Psalm 42:4*
and my prayer rose to you,	
to your holy temple.	*Psalm 18:6*
"Those who cling to worthless idols	*Psalm 31:6*
turn away from God's love for them.	
But I, with shouts of grateful praise,	
will sacrifice to you.	*Psalm 50:14*
What I have vowed I will make good.	
I will say, 'Salvation comes from the LORD.'"[18]	*Psalm 3:8*

Many people have found comfort, strength, encouragement, and blessing by not only reading the Psalms but also praying them—consciously making the words of the psalmist their own. A friend of mine was terrified of tunnels in general and the Lincoln Tunnel (which burrows for one and a half miles under the Hudson River between New Jersey and New York) in particular. Unfortunately, her responsibilities required her to ride a bus through that tunnel at least twice a week, sometimes more. Usually she would take out a small Bible and read and pray Psalm 23 for the duration of the trip through the tunnel.

Benedictine monks, who follow the ancient Rule of St. Benedict, pray aloud through the book of Psalms—all 150 of them—every two weeks in the course of their "hours" of worship.

You may want to pray a psalm a day (except, perhaps, for Psalm 119, which is the longest). Or you might pray a psalm in the morning and another at night. You may want to pray Psalm 27 when you are afraid:

> *The LORD is my light and my salvation;*
> *whom shall I fear?*
> *The LORD is the stronghold of my life;*
> *of whom shall I be afraid?* [19]

You may choose to pray Psalm 42 when you are discouraged or depressed:

> *Why are you cast down, O my soul,*
> *and why are you in turmoil within me?*
> *Hope in God; for I shall again praise him,*
> *my salvation and my God.* [20]

Psalm 1 can help you pray for wisdom and righteousness

in your life. Psalm 19 can help you praise God. Psalm 52 can aid your confession and repentance. Psalm 138 can help you express gratitude. "When we pray the Psalms," Eugene Peterson says, "we pray through all the parts of our lives and our history and cover the ground of our intricate implication in sin."[21] Praying the Psalms enlarges our prayer vocabulary, teaching us to pray the gamut of human experience. It gives us words for otherwise inexpressible thoughts and feelings. It gives us permission to say things we might otherwise never say. And over time—as it apparently did for Jonah in the fish's belly and Jesus on the cross—it stores within us a catalog of prayers to call upon in dark, confusing, or devastating times.

PRAY THE PRAYERS OF THE BIBLE

If you pray the Lord's Prayer, you already pray at least one of the prayers found in the Bible. And if you pray the Psalms, you are mining the richest prayer vein ever known to humanity. But there are many more prayers in the Bible that can aid your praying and many that can provide help when you're not sure what to pray.

When my friend entered hospice care, for example, I wasn't sure whether I should pray for miraculous healing or for a quick and smooth transition into heaven. So I told God about my mixed feelings and expressed my possibly selfish desire—that my friend be quickly and fully restored to health, adding the prayer of Jesus in Gethsemane: "Nevertheless, not as I will, but as you will."[22]

Sometimes when I am asked to pray for someone without

knowing any details about his or her need, I will pray Ephesians 3:14–21 (changing the pronouns from "you" to "him" or "her," or inserting the person's name):

> *For this reason I bow my knees before the Father, from whom every family in heaven and on earth is named, that according to the riches of his glory he may grant you to be strengthened with power through his Spirit in your inner being, so that Christ may dwell in your hearts through faith—that you, being rooted and grounded in love, may have strength to comprehend with all the saints what is the breadth and length and height and depth, and to know the love of Christ that surpasses knowledge, that you may be filled with all the fullness of God.*
>
> *Now to him who is able to do far more abundantly than all that we ask or think, according to the power at work within us, to him be glory in the church and in Christ Jesus throughout all generations, forever and ever. Amen.*[23]

Or I may pray Paul's prayer for enlightenment in Colossians 1 (again altering the pronouns):

> *Asking that you may be filled with the knowledge of his will in all spiritual wisdom and understanding, so as to walk in a manner worthy of the Lord, fully pleasing to him, bearing fruit in every good work and increasing in the knowledge of God. May you be strengthened with all*

power, according to his glorious might, for all endurance and patience with joy, giving thanks to the Father, who has qualified you to share in the inheritance of the saints in light.[24]

Other Bible prayers you can pray include the early church's prayer for boldness (Acts 4:29–30), Aaron's prayer for blessing (Numbers 6:24–26), Habakkuk's prayer for revival (Habakkuk 3:2), Jabez's prayer for influence (1 Chronicles 4:10), and the tax collector's prayer for mercy (Luke 18:13).

These and many other Bible prayers make it easier to pray according to God's will. They can help you express yourself when words fail. And they can simultaneously enrich your knowledge of the Bible, confidence in prayer, and sensitivity to the Spirit of God as you pray.

PRAY THE PROMISES OF GOD

"There are general promises and principles laid down in the Bible," said evangelist Charles Finney, "that Christians might make use of if they would only *think*. Whenever you are in circumstances to which the promises or principles apply, you are to use them."[25] He gives an example:

Suppose it is a time when wickedness prevails, and you are led to pray for God's interference. What promise do you have? This one: "When the enemy shall come in like a flood, the Spirit of the LORD shall lift up a standard against him" (Isaiah 59:19 KJV). Here you see a general promise, laying down a principle of God's administration, which you may apply to the case before you as a warrant for exercising faith in prayer. And if the inquiry is made as to the time in which God will grant blessings in answer to prayer, you have this promise: "While they are still speaking I will hear" (Isaiah 65:24 KJV).[26]

So pray the promises. Confess your sins and claim the promise of forgiveness (1 John 1:9). Tell God what you need and claim His provision (Philippians 4:19). Ask God to show you a way to escape from temptation (1 Corinthians 10:13). Ask Him for comfort (2 Corinthians 1:2–4). Ask Him for wisdom (James 1:5). Ask for His presence (Matthew 18:20; 28:20). Ask for peace (John 14:27).

Not every promise in scripture is applicable today (for example, God told Abraham that his descendants would be as numerous as the stars; that promise does not apply to everyone who reads it). But there are so many promises in the Bible that do apply to you and me—and can be prayed as Finney says—that we can pray them with faith, hope, and joy.

PRAY AS YOU READ

I have been praying the Bible for decades now, and it has not only enriched my prayer life and increased my Bible knowledge but also has drawn me closer to God than I ever imagined I could be (prayer in general has a way of doing that, but praying the Bible, in particular, will do it). In a previous book, *Quit Going to Church*, I tried to describe how I often pray as I read:

I might actually start out my reading with Moses's prayer [in Exodus 33:15–16], and whether I'm going to read a few chapters or just a verse or two, whether I'm going to read a psalm or one of those long genealogies, I might start out by praying, "Lord, teach me your ways so I may know you."

Then I might read a passage like this one in Exodus 33, where Moses said to God, "If your Presence does not go with us, do not send us up from here."

And I might stop there, and say, "Lord, I want your presence more than anything. I want to spend time with you. I want to know that I've been in your presence. I want other people to know, when I leave here, that I've been in your presence. I want to carry the fragrance of your presence with me throughout this day, so please come to me now in such a way that our conversation will not end when I leave this place, but that every step I take will be taken in communion with you."

Or I might just as likely read that passage where Moses says to God, "If your Presence does not go with us, do not send us up from here," and I might pause to say, "Lord, you know I haven't felt your presence for some time now. What's that about? Where have you been? It's not like I haven't been faithful. It's not like I haven't plopped myself down in this prayer chair day after day. And yet still I'm exhausted. I feel empty—and you seem absent. So if you're going to keep this up, then please tell me."

In the next breath, I might stop for a moment, and say, "Yes, Lord, I do believe you are present even when I don't feel you. I know that—in my head—and I know you want me to be faithful even when I don't feel your presence. But I have enough faith to believe my presence brings you joy, because your Word says so. It says you delight in me. . .so can you help me feel some of that—in my heart? Can you please give me a sense of your pleasure?"

Then I might stop reading, or I might go on in this chapter, to the next couple of verses, and read: "And the LORD said to Moses, 'I will do the very thing you have asked, because I am pleased with you and I know you by name.' Then Moses said, 'Now show me your glory.' "

And I might say, "Oh, Lord, if you would do that. . .if you would show me your glory, I would be so grateful. That's what I need, Lord. Show me your glory. Show me your presence. Show me your hand on my life. Show me I'm loved."[27]

Praying biblically, as Jesus did, is a path to immense blessing and fulfillment in prayer. It unites you in prayer, not only with psalmists and prophets, but also with the Lord Jesus Christ Himself. It can do for you something like what it did for two young Mexican women, as Wesley and Stacey Campbell describe in their book *Praying the Bible: The Pathway to Spirituality*:

A few years ago, we were ministering in the mountains of Puebla, which is about a four-hour drive from Mexico City. The situation was most desperate. The Indians of the area lived in villages built atop mountain peaks a mile high in the air, which meant that in order to get water, the villagers had to walk a mile straight down to the valley below. These villagers were descendants of the ancient Inca and Aztec tribes. Warring factions had driven these people to build on the very tops of the mountains in order to protect themselves from their enemies. Farming was difficult and life was very harsh. Today alcoholism is rampant and violence and abuse are epidemic. It hardly seemed the place for two single Mexican señoritas to start church planting. Yet these two girls had braved the odds and seen scores of village Indians come to Christ and be baptized. At the end of one long day of preaching, one of these young church planters came up to me to give a testimony.

"You will not remember me," she said, "but I was in one of your meetings in Mexico City. At that conference you taught about praying the Bible. You were talking about the missionaries of old and how the Celtic monks prayed the whole book of Psalms every week. Since the conference was called 'The Revolution,' you told us to 'pray the whole book of Psalms every week, for a number of months, and a revolution will take place in your life.'" Beaming, she continued, "I began to do this. Six months later I gave up my practice as an accountant and here I am. I wouldn't be doing anything else. Thank you for teaching me to pray the Bible." Driving down the mountains that night, I realized afresh the power of praying the Bible. It changes the lives of those who do it and the lives of those they touch.[28]

Lord, Your Word vaults across the skies
   from sunrise to sunset,
melting ice, scorching deserts,
   warming hearts to faith.
Your revelation, God, is whole
   and pulls our lives together.
The signposts You give are clear
   and point out the right road.
The life maps You provide are right,
   showing the way to joy.
All Your directions are plain
   and easy on the eyes.
Your reputation is twenty-four-carat gold,
   with a lifetime guarantee.
Your decisions, God, are accurate
   down to the nth degree.
Your Word is better than a diamond,
   better than a diamond set between emeralds.
I love it more than strawberries in spring,
   better than red, ripe strawberries.
And more: Your Word warns me of danger
   and directs me to hidden treasure.
Otherwise how will I find my way?
   Or know when I play the fool?
Clean the slate, God, so I can start the day fresh!
   Keep me from stupid sins,
   from thinking I can take over Your work;
Then I can start each new day sun-washed,
   scrubbed clean of the grime of sin.
These are the words in my mouth;

these are what I chew on and pray.
Accept them when I place them
    on the morning altar,
O God, my Altar-Rock,
    God, Priest-of-My-Altar.[29] Amen.

17

PRAY PERSISTENTLY

~

I mentioned earlier that I am a lifelong Cincinnati Reds fan. I've persevered with my team through the good, bad, and ugly—through the glory days of "The Big Red Machine," the strike-shortened 1981 season (when the Reds boasted the best record in baseball yet failed to make the playoffs), and the horrific 1982 season (when the Reds lost 101 games, qualifying for the *worst* record in baseball).

I also mentioned a recent Reds game that my wife, Robin, and I attended at Great American Ballpark. It was a memorable game for several reasons. The Reds jumped out to an 8–0 lead in the first two innings. By the seventh inning, they still led, 9–5, when Jose "Jumbo" Diaz entered the game.

It seemed obvious that a healthy percentage of the crowd that night knew Jumbo's story because his entry into the game generated enthusiastic applause. He signed as a Los Angeles Dodgers prospect in 2001 and played the next season for the (minor league) Gulf Coast Dodgers, the South Georgia Waves, and the Great Falls Dodgers. He appeared in only seven games in 2003 for the Ogden Raptors and South Georgia Waves. In 2004 he pitched in thirty-seven games for the Columbus Catfish and Vero Beach Dodgers. In 2005, 2006, and 2007, he played for (respectively) the Gulf Coast Dodgers, Vero Beach Dodgers, Gulf Coast Dodgers, Vero Beach Dodgers, Jacksonville (FL) Suns, and Great Lakes Loons. Tommy John surgery kept him off the field in 2008, but in 2009 (after signing a new contract with the Texas Rangers) he played for the Frisco (TX) RoughRiders. When the Rangers released him, he signed a new contract with the Baltimore Orioles and played for the Frederick (MD) Keys and the Bowie (MD) Baysox. In 2011, he pitched for Bowie and the Norfolk (IL) Tides. After signing with the Pittsburgh Pirates for 2012, he pitched in forty-one games for the Indianapolis Indians. He joined the Cincinnati Reds' farm system in 2013 and pitched in forty-four games that year with the Louisville Bats. Though his 2013 performance earned him an invitation to the Reds' big league camp in spring training, where he pitched well, he was one of the last players to be cut before opening day. He started 2014 in Louisville, his thirteenth year in the minor leagues.

He had pitched in 340 games for four different baseball organizations. He had changed teams nineteen times. He was eighteen years old when he signed with the Dodgers and turned thirty in his first spring training with the Reds.

But on June 20, 2014, Diaz got the call. He joined the Reds in Cincinnati and entered that evening's game against the Toronto Blue Jays in the seventh inning. And had a disastrous outing, giving up two homers and three runs in one inning.

Many would have given up long before. Maybe after posting a bloated 6.64 ERA (earned run average) in 2003. Maybe after a rotator cuff injury. Maybe after coming so close to "the show," only to be sent back to the minor leagues just before the season started. Or maybe after his terrible, horrible, no good, very bad major league debut. But Diaz never gave up.

He told reporters in the Reds' clubhouse, "You have some point where you wake up and say, 'I'm working hard every day and I don't get the call.' You have to fight it, because you never know when that call will come. . . . If I didn't get the call, I did the best I can. Thank you God, I got the call this morning."[1]

Diaz finished his rookie season with the Reds at the age of thirty. After giving up two home runs in his first major league inning pitched, he gave up only one more the rest of the season. He appeared in thirty-six games and posted a respectable 3.38 ERA.

UNTIL THE ANSWER COMES

If Jumbo Diaz can persevere through more than a decade of disappointment before reaching his dream of pitching in the major leagues, why do we find it so hard to keep praying for the same people, the same needs, the same things, day after day, without giving up? Why is it so difficult to keep going until we "get the call," until the answer comes?

One reason may be that we are lazy. Andrew Murray, in his classic *With Christ in the School of Prayer*, suggested:

> *When our repeated prayers remain unanswered, it is easy for our lazy flesh—maintaining the appearance of pious submission—to think that we must stop praying because God may have a secret reason for withholding His answer to our request. Faith alone can overcome difficulty. Once faith has taken its stand on God's Word and the Name of Jesus, and has yielded itself to the leading of the Spirit to seek only God's will and honor in its prayer, it need not be discouraged by delay. It knows from Scripture that the power of believing prayer is considerable; real faith can never be disappointed. It*

> *knows that to exercise its power, it must be gathered up,*
> *just like water, until the stream can come down in full*
> *force. Prayer must often be "heaped up" until God sees*
> *that its measure is full.*[2]

Another possible reason we are no Jumbo Diaz when it comes to prayer is that we are busy—or think we are. We fill our lives with working, meeting, eating, drinking, sleeping, driving, talking, listening, reading, entertaining (or being entertained), and so on, until there is no room for the things we say really matter. Yes, our schedules are full and our souls are empty, but there's no time to pray for them to be otherwise. Yes, our marriages are in trouble, but time for prayer is so hard to find. Yes, our children are struggling, but we've done all we can think of to do, except persevere in prayer. And so it goes. Peter Kreeft wrote:

> *[We think] that prayer is a waste of time. Brother*
> *Lawrence recognizes this, and says, "At first one often*
> *thinks it lost time. But you must go on, and resolve to*
> *persevere in it to death" (Letter 6). For our relationship*
> *to God is the whole meaning and point of all our time.*
> *We must give the loaves and fishes of our time (that is,*
> *our life, our life-time) to him, for only he, the Creator*
> *and Master of time, can save and multiply the time we*
> *give him, just as he multiplied the little boy's loaves and*
> *fishes (Jn 6).*[3]

At the most fundamental level, we find it hard to persevere in prayer because we are not yet truly or fully followers of

Jesus. We don't quite believe Him when He makes it clear that we "ought always to pray and not lose heart."[4] Because if we believe what Jesus says, and follow Him in doing what He tells us to do, we will do at least the following three things.

PRAY UNTIL GOD ANSWERS

Jesus repeatedly urged His followers not only to pray but also to pray desperately, insistently, and persistently. In Luke's account, Jesus paired the Lord's Prayer with an illustration about a friend who would not be denied:

> *[Jesus] said to them, "Which of you who has a friend will go to him at midnight and say to him, 'Friend, lend me three loaves, for a friend of mine has arrived on a journey, and I have nothing to set before him'; and he will answer from within, 'Do not bother me; the door is now shut, and my children are with me in bed. I cannot get up and give you anything'? I tell you, though he will not get up and give him anything because he is his friend, yet because of his impudence he will rise and give him whatever he needs. And I tell you, ask, and it will be given to you; seek, and you will find; knock, and it will be opened to you."* [5]

The point Jesus made in that story is lost a little in most translations. He is not suggesting that God is anything like the sleeping friend who "will not get up and give him anything because he is his friend" but will do so to get rid of a nuisance. On the contrary, the comparison is between you and the guy at the door, the friend who asks for bread (just as the Lord's

Prayer asks for bread). You must keep asking and seeking and knocking until you get what you need.

In fact, the Greek wording of verse 9 ("ask, and it will be given to you," etc.) uses a verb form that makes that point crystal clear. Bible scholar William Barclay wrote:

> In Greek there are two kinds of imperative; there is the aorist imperative which issues one definite command. "Shut the door behind you" would be an aorist imperative. There is the present imperative which issues a command that a man should always do something or should go on doing something. "Always shut doors behind you" would be a present imperative. The imperatives here are present imperatives; therefore Jesus is saying, "Go on asking; go on seeking; go on knocking." He is telling us to persist in prayer; he is telling us never to be discouraged in prayer.[6]

Jesus is saying, "Be the same person in prayer that you would be at the door of your neighbor. Keep asking. Keep seeking. Keep knocking. Be shamelessly persistent—undeniable—in praying, and you will receive and find and have the door opened to you."

PRAY UNTIL GOD CHANGES YOUR PRAYER

Only once did the Gospel writer Luke explain the gist of one of Jesus' parables. He wrote, "Then Jesus told his disciples a parable to show them that they should always pray and not give up."[7] That parable is known as the parable of the persistent widow:

*"There was once a judge in some city who never gave
God a thought and cared nothing for people. A widow
in that city kept after him: 'My rights are being violated.
Protect me!'*

*"He never gave her the time of day. But after this
went on and on he said to himself, 'I care nothing
what God thinks, even less what people think. But
because this widow won't quit badgering me, I'd better
do something and see that she gets justice—otherwise
I'm going to end up beaten black-and-blue by her
pounding.'"*

*Then the Master said, "Do you hear what that
judge, corrupt as he is, is saying? So what makes you
think God won't step in and work justice for his chosen
people, who continue to cry out for help? Won't he stick
up for them? I assure you, he will. He will not drag his
feet. But how much of that kind of persistent faith will
the Son of Man find on the earth when he returns?"*[8]

Jesus' parable does not *equate* the judge with God but *contrasts*
the two. However, like the story of the friend at midnight,
Jesus is saying that you and I should act like the widow.
We should be that persistent in prayer. We should "keep on
asking. . .keep on seeking, and. . .keep on knocking."[9]

But notice that Jesus also mentions the importance of
faith in such perseverance. As *The Message* paraphrase puts it,
he asks, "How much of that kind of persistent faith will the
Son of Man find on the earth when he returns?"[10] Persistence
in prayer takes faith.

Andrew Murray wrote:

Don't let delay shake your faith, for it is faith that will provide the answer in time. Each believing prayer is a step nearer to the final victory! It ripens the fruit, conquers hindrances in the unseen world, and hastens the end. Child of God! Give the Father time! . . . He wants your blessing to be rich, full, and sure. Give Him time, but continue praying day and night.[11]

Your faith, however, must be faith in the Father, not faith in the answer. The faith that perseveres is faith in the greatness and goodness of God. It is faith in His willingness to answer prayer. It is faith in the wisdom of His timing. It is faith in His good intentions toward you and the subject of your prayer.

This kind of faith will move mountains, but it is capable of moving you as well. It will sometimes change your circumstances. It will sometimes change your prayer.

You may ask God to "call down fire"[12] on those who attack or abuse you, but He may change your prayer into one for a heart of love and compassion for yourself. You may beg God to heal you from sickness, but He may transform your prayer and soon have you asking Him to bring glory to Himself through your illness. You may ask for a raise and soon find yourself praying for a whole new career instead.

Sometimes when this happens, God will grant both the initial request and the revised request. My son, Aaron, was considering an attractive job offer in a different (and distant) state, where the cost of living was much greater and the culture quite different. When the position was first presented to him, he prayed for God to keep him calm and rational as he considered the possibility. As he underwent multiple interviews, he prayed for freedom from fear and anxiety. Soon his praying changed as the process continued, and he prayed largely for him and his wife to be on the same page when the time came to decide. As God seemed to be answering that prayer, he asked for a financial package that would more than meet their needs. When that was answered, he and his wife prayed for their children to be excited about the opportunity and, finally, for their extended family to be supportive. Over a period of four months, Aaron says his prayer changed many times—sometimes because his prayers were being answered and other times because he was becoming wiser.

PRAY UNTIL GOD CHANGES YOU

E. M. Bounds once wrote, "Prayer in its highest form and grandest success assumes the attitude of a wrestler with God. It is the contest, trial and victory of faith; a victory not secured from an enemy, but from Him who tries our faith that He may enlarge it: that tests our strength to make us stronger."[13]

Remember Jacob? The first book of the Bible tells his story. Jacob and his brother, Esau, were twins. And even before they were born—while they were still in the womb—they were fighting, jockeying for position. Jacob was a mama's boy, and Esau was his dad's favorite.

When their father was on his deathbed, Jacob tricked his father into giving him the inheritance that was supposed to go to Esau, simultaneously defrauding both his father and his brother. When Esau found out, he started plotting to kill his brother, so Jacob packed up and left home. On his mother's advice, he fled to the home of a distant uncle, where he got married—twice!—had children, and prospered in business, until he had to get out of town quick again because this time his uncle was after him.

So Jacob and his wives and his children and his flocks had nowhere to go but back home. . .where his brother Esau would be, the brother he had betrayed, the brother he had cheated, the brother who might still want to kill him.

So he devised an elaborate scheme and sent messengers to his brother, with the word that Jacob was coming home and he hoped Esau would be happy to see him. And those messengers returned with the news that Esau was coming to meet Jacob. . .along with four hundred men!

Jacob's response at hearing that was something along the lines of "Aye yi yi!"

So he divided his caravan into two groups, hoping if one was attacked, the other could make a clean getaway. He sent a string of messengers ahead, each with gifts of goats and camels and cows and donkeys to butter up his brother. And he settled down for a restless night in camp.

Little did he know how restless his night would be.

Well before daybreak, he sent his family and the last of his possessions ahead, and he stayed in camp alone. And there, the Bible says, Someone "wrestled with him until the breaking of the day."[14] They locked arms. They locked wills. Neither one would let the other go. Even after Jacob's hip was dislocated, they continued the contest.

Finally, when Jacob's Opponent suggested that Jacob should give up, as the day was coming to an end—which meant his dreaded reunion with his brother was approaching fast—Jacob answered, "I will not let you go unless you bless me."[15]

"Say your name."

"Jacob."

"No longer Jacob," his Opponent said, "but 'Fights-with-God,' for you have wrestled with God. . .and won."

Then Jacob asked again, and received the blessing he sought. His reunion with his brother, Esau, was a happy one, but from that day on, Jacob limped. His prayer session had changed *him*.

So it may often be with you. You may want more than anything for God to change others. You may pray fervently and persistently for Him to change your circumstances. But He may decide instead (or sometimes, in addition) to change *you*. So keep praying. Be persistent. Never give up until God answers, until He changes your prayer, or until He changes *you*.

N. T. Wright has written:

God is working like an artist with difficult material; and prayer is the way some of that material co-operates with the artist instead of resisting him. How that is so we shall never fully understand until we see God face to face. That it is so is one of the most basic Christian insights.

So, treat God as a father, and let him know how things are with you! Ask, search, and knock and see what happens! Expect some surprises on the way, but don't expect that God will ever let you down.[16]

Gracious God, my Father,
*   forgive me for the many times I have finished praying long before You have started answering.*
*   Forgive me for losing faith and losing hope.*

Forgive me for misinterpreting Your wise timing as rejection or refusal.

Make me like the friend at midnight, who goes on asking, seeking, and knocking until the request is granted.

Make me like the persistent widow who will not be denied.

Make me like Jacob, who wrestled with You and won, not because You were reluctant but because You had in mind all along to bring about a change in him.

Teach me to be shamelessly persistent—undeniable—in praying, until I receive and find and have the door opened.

In Jesus' name, amen.

18

PRAY BOLDLY

~

Among my two-and-a-half-year-old grandson Ryder's most frequent words are these: "I want some of that."

I plop a toasted and buttered breakfast bagel on my plate. He says, "I want some of that."

I carve up a promising seedless watermelon. He says, "I want some of that."

I unwrap a Hostess chocolate cupcake. Suddenly he appears beside me. "I want some of that."

I tote in a plate of sizzling hamburgers and hot dogs from the grill. He says, "I want some of that."

Yes, I know I'm giving the impression that I am constantly eating. But that's not my point. My point is that he never hesitates to ask, not even for a second. If he even suspects that I have something tasty in my hands (which, because I *am* constantly eating, happens a lot), he asks. He asks quickly. He asks boldly. He asks without reservation, without any fear that he will be denied.

And you know what? He's right. I remind him to say please, of course—because who wants a hooligan for a grandson?—but I never deny him. I don't make him earn it. I don't make him beg. I don't quickly gobble it down and tell him it's all gone. When he says, "I want some of that," I grant his request.

Ryder's approach is endorsed by Jesus. He said:

"Keep on asking, and you will receive what you ask for.
Keep on seeking, and you will find. Keep on knocking,

230 — BOB HOSTETLER

and the door will be opened to you. For everyone who asks, receives. Everyone who seeks, finds. And to everyone who knocks, the door will be opened.

"You parents—if your children ask for a loaf of bread, do you give them a stone instead? Or if they ask for a fish, do you give them a snake? Of course not! So if you sinful people know how to give good gifts to your children, how much more will your heavenly Father give good gifts to those who ask him." [1]

Notice that Jesus chose two of the most common, everyday requests a child might make of a father or mother in those days. Mom pulls some warm flatbread from the oven: "I want some of that." Dad strips a morsel from the roasting fish on the spit: "I want some of that." What parent would deny a hungry child? Who in their right mind would substitute a stone or a snake in such an event?

The point Jesus makes is, "How much more?" How much more loving and kind is your heavenly Father? How much more certain is He to answer your requests? How much more gracious and giving and generous is He? How much more willing? Wealthy? Wise?

FIG TREES AND MOUNTAINS

The Gospel writer Mark relates an incident that happened one day as Jesus and His closest followers were on their way into the city of Jerusalem. He says that Jesus saw "a fig tree in leaf" [2] and went to it to see if it had any young figs to eat. When He saw that there were none, "He said to it, 'May no one ever eat fruit from you again.'" [3]

The next morning, as He and His disciples made the same trek into the city, "They saw the fig tree withered away to its roots." Peter remarked on it to Jesus, as though He or anyone should be surprised. But Jesus said:

> *"Have faith in God. Truly, I say to you, whoever says*
> *to this mountain, 'Be taken up and thrown into the*
> *sea,' and does not doubt in his heart, but believes that*
> *what he says will come to pass, it will be done for him.*
> *Therefore I tell you, whatever you ask in prayer, believe*
> *that you have received it, and it will be yours."* [4]

There is so much going on in that passage, and so much to study and think about. But for our purposes here and now, I want to focus on perhaps the most straightforward and easy-to-understand part of the whole story. When Peter expressed amazement at the withered fig tree, Jesus could have responded any number of ways.

He might have said, "I know, I got a little grumpy yesterday when there were no young figs on the tree. My bad."

He might have answered Peter, "Let that be a lesson to you: Don't cross Me when I'm hungry."

He might have said, "I hope one of you will write this down later, so people will know how important it is to be fruitful, in season or out of season."

But of course, He said none of those things (and I'm not suggesting you take any of those possibilities seriously). Instead, Jesus turned the whole fig tree incident into a lesson on prayer. In fact, my paraphrase of His exchange with Peter goes something like this:

"Rabbi! Look at that! The fig tree you cursed is all withered."

"Of course it is, Peter. Sheesh, have some faith in God! A fig tree is nothing; if you had the faith, and the boldness, you could pray for this mountain right here[5] to be thrown into the sea—thirty-some miles away— and it would happen! The question is not will a fig tree wither at your word or a mountain move at your command; the question is, will you ask for it in prayer and believe that your Father will do it?"

That was Jesus' word to Peter: *believe.* Believe in a "how much more" God. Believe in His mountain-moving power. Believe that God is listening and ready to act. Believe enough to "come boldly unto the throne of grace, that we may obtain mercy, and find grace to help in time of need."[6]

PRAY WITH FAITH

Jesus may have had an advantage—being the incarnate Son of God—but He clearly and boldly stated that His followers could do anything He did—and more. He said:

"Truly, truly, I say to you, whoever believes in me will also do the works that I do; and greater works than these will he do, because I am going to the Father. Whatever you ask in my name, this I will do, that the Father may be glorified in the Son."[7]

Greater than cursing a fig tree and making it wither? Apparently so (see Acts 5:1–10).

Greater than healing a paralyzed man? Apparently so (see Acts 3:1–11).

Greater than raising a widow's son from the dead? Apparently so (see Acts 9:36–41).

Apparently that first generation of Jesus' followers took His promises seriously. They prayed for boldness (Acts 4:29). They prayed for prisoners to be released (Acts 12:5). They prayed for the sick to be healed (Acts 28:8). They prayed for the dead to be raised (Acts 9:40). And God answered their prayers!

If Jesus meant what He said, then we have every reason to pray boldly, believingly, even brashly. Twentieth-century writer and preacher Samuel Logan Brengle wrote:

God loves to be compelled. God will be compelled by persistent prayer and faith. I imagine God is often grieved and disappointed and angry with us, as the prophet was with the king who struck the ground three times rather than five or six (2 Kings 13:18–19), because we ask so little.

The woman who came to Jesus to have the devil cast out of her daughter puts most Christians to shame. She would not be turned away. At first, Jesus answered her not a word, and so He often treats us today. We pray and get no answer. God is silent. Then Jesus rebuffed her. That would have been enough to make blaspheming skeptics of most modern folks. Not so with her. Her desperate faith grew sublime. At last, Jesus declared, "It is not right to take the children's bread and throw it to the dogs."

> *Then the woman's faith compelled Him, for she said, "Yes, Lord, yet even the dogs eat the crumbs that fall from their masters' table."*
>
> *She was willing to receive the dogs' portion. Oh, how her faith triumphed, and Jesus, amazed, said, "Great is your faith! Be it done for you as you desire" (Matthew 15:21–28). Jesus meant to bless her all the time, if her faith would hold out. And so He means to bless you.*[8]

Praying with faith means *don't be timid*. "Come boldly to the throne of grace,"[9] the author of Hebrews wrote. Remember Esther's story? She took her life in her hands and marched into King Ahasuerus's throne room to make life-changing, world-altering requests of him. His was hardly a "throne of grace," yet she threw off all caution and gained what she asked—what she and all her people needed. We should do no less, especially since our king is gracious, merciful, and generous.

Praying with faith means *don't try to hedge your bets*. Sometimes—particularly in worship services and prayer meetings, where others can hear us praying—we try to "hedge our bets," so to speak. We may pray, "Lord, heal sister Jackie, but if not, make her comfortable." That's hardly mountain-moving faith. We should always strive to pray prayers that align with God's priorities ("May Your name be kept holy; may Your kingdom come; may Your will be done"), but faith doesn't hedge a bet. It goes out on a limb. It presses through the crowd to touch the hem of the Master's garment. It strikes the arrow on the ground over and over and over and over. It asks for even the crumbs from the master's table.

Praying with faith means *don't try to protect God from embarrassment.* Do you tend to pray for realistic answers to prayer? Do you ask for likely outcomes? Or do you pray mountain-moving prayers? Do you pray for things that couldn't possibly happen unless God clearly intervenes? Sometimes I think well-meaning Christians try to protect God from embarrassment. You know, if we pray, "Heal now, or heal in heaven," we can say that God answered our prayer even if Sister Jackie dies. Shame on us. Jesus said, "Have faith in God. Truly, I say to you, whoever says to this mountain, 'Be taken up and thrown into the sea,' and does not doubt in his heart, but believes that what he says will come to pass, it will be done for him."[10]

PRAY WITH DESPERATION

My friend Cindy Sproles faced a desperate situation that could only be resolved through prayer. I will let her tell the story:

The nightmare started with a phone message: "They've arrested me. Mom, help me." My husband and I were twelve hundred miles away, and I was expected to speak at a Christian conference.

Prayer is never a waste of time, and in my own inability to find the right words, I found myself pouring out the same petition: Oh, God, my Savior. . .have favor over my son, over Your child.

Praying for others usually comes easy to me, but praying for myself was staggering. It wasn't that I felt too good to present my needs before the Father. Rather, the needs of others always seemed much greater than my own. That is, until now. Now it was my turn. My son's turn. And I was speechless, unsure how to pray for my own.

The adage "Desperate times call for desperate measures" rang true as I walked onto the platform at the conference and publicly laid out my son's needs. "Please pray for my son. I need you to pray for him because I can't do anything to help him. I can't go to him. I can't. . .can't fix things."

I'm convinced God handpicked the man who stepped to the front, placed his bear-sized arm around me, and prayed the most heartfelt and healing prayer I've ever experienced. His words lifted to heaven like a sweet aroma, and their meaning soaked my heart like a soothing spring rain. This man, along with four other individuals, would form an unbreakable prayer ring over the ensuing months.

As the months dragged by, court date after court date washed over us like ocean waves, rising to nearly drown us. With each answered prayer the waves subsided, retreating back into the depths, waiting for the next tide. Morning and night, countless times throughout the day, I dropped to my knees, calling on God for mercy. Repeatedly through e-mail and Facebook, I called on my prayer posse, who offered no judgment on me or my child but faithfully and fervently prayed the need. Their faithfulness gave us strength.

Just weeks before the final court date, I led a Bible study on 2 Chronicles 20, the story of King Jehoshaphat and how his kingdom was about to be attacked. Jehoshaphat called the people together—men, women, and children. They prayed and waited. God sent a prophet to tell them the battle was not theirs but His. He had already fought it and won.

The story bound itself to my heart, and I did as Jehoshaphat had done. I called together everyone I knew, hundreds, and asked them to pray and claim the story of King Jehoshaphat—pray God would fight this battle for my child before he entered the courtroom. And they did. This unbreakable circle of friends grew into hundreds of men, women, and children who stood shoulder-to-shoulder and prayed. . .and waited.

In the courtroom, however, our child faced a decision: Make a false plea and accept a consequence for something he didn't do, or tell the truth. . .and face even worse punishment. The state's attorney pushed for punishment. We sobbed with our son on the phone and the decision was made: accept a plea.

When my son finally called, his voice was filled with joy. "You won't believe this, Mom. It was a miracle." He said that—for the first time—he had been allowed to speak in the courtroom. He was given an opportunity to explain. . .and the judge listened! Though there was still a small consequence, the complete reversal of a stubborn prosecution stunned the court. When the gavel struck the bench, our son walked away from a battle that had been won for him.

I once heard faith compared in three facets. There is faith—hoping God will do what He promises. Then

there is strong faith—believing God will do what He
promises. But great faith is knowing God has already
done what He promised, long before the result is seen.

God did not stop the process for our son, and neither
did He prevent all the consequences, but without a
doubt He showed up and cleaned up a situation that
could have ended badly. Every word lifted to our Abba
Father was heard and answered in His time. There is
power in the prayers of God's children—amazing power
in the prayer that is girded in faith, grounded in trust,
and desperate enough to never let go.

We often ask people to pray with us. We try to get as many people praying as possible, perhaps because we think God is more likely to answer when more people pray. And there is probably something to that (see Matthew 18:19). But I think something different is at work in cases like Cindy's. I don't think more people praying necessarily moves God to action; I think we get more people to pray when we are most desperate for answers. And God answers desperate prayer. God answers bold prayer. God answers prayer that will hold on and not give up until He answers.

PRAY WITH IMAGINATION

Jesus' disciples were clearly surprised when He cursed a fig tree. Who does that? Who responds to such a situation with words that alter the future?

Those first followers of Jesus were probably also surprised when He talked about praying in such a way as to move the very mountain under their feet. And casting it into the sea?

What a mind! What an imagination!

But guess what? That's the very kind of praying Jesus recommends to His followers. Not only then, but also today—and specifically and especially when we pray. I recently heard another friend of mine, Greg Stier of Dare2Share,[11] tell this story at a conference in Florida:

> *About fourteen years ago I was in Washington, DC.*
> *I'd been invited to this thing called the Youth Ministry*
> *Executive Council. And there were ministry leaders from*
> *all over the nation gathering together, about thirty or*
> *forty of them, to strategize about how to reach the next*
> *generation. There were Baptists, there were parachurch*
> *organizations, there were mainline denominations, and*
> *there were Pentecostal churches.*
>
> *We all at one point broke up into small groups*
> *to pray. And somehow, I got stuck at the Pentecostal*
> *table. I was saved in a Baptist church, raised in a Bible*
> *church. I myself am not Pentecostal. But I'm at the*
> *Pentecostal table. And Pentecostals pray loudly. And I*
> *wasn't used to that.*
>
> *And the leader of the parade was a guy named Bob.*
> *And Bob was a little like Elvis. He was dressed to the*
> *nines, and he had perfect TV preacher hair. He'd been*
> *on CBN, TBN—you name a "BN," he'd been on it.*
>
> *And he's like, "All right, everybody." He reminded*
> *me of Elvis. He goes, "We're going to pray. You guys*
> *ready to pray? Because we're going to pray. We're going to*
> *start with you, and we're going to go over to you." That*
> *was me. I was the last guy.*

He looks at the guy to his left and says, "What's your prayer request?"

He says, "I want to claim a million souls for the kingdom."

Bob says, "Let's claim it. Claim it now." And they go for it. They're all praying. They're all saying, "Amen!"

And I'm kind of embarrassed, to be honest with you. Because all the other tables are pretty quiet, and our table is getting louder and louder. But I want to participate, so every once in a while, I say, "Make it so, Lord."

And he's going around the table and they're getting louder and louder and louder, and they're coming around to me. They're all praying for their ministries, so I'm thinking, Maybe if I pray for something personal, it'll keep them quiet.

It gets to me and he goes, "What's your prayer request?"

I said, "You know, my wife and I have been married for ten years, and we can't have kids. So can you pray that we have kids?"

He goes, "Oh, that's an easy one. I've prayed for hundreds of couples. They've never failed to have kids! Gather 'round, boys!"

They all stand up. They come out of their chairs. I'm like, No no no no no no no no. They place their hands on my head (thank the Lord!). And he starts praying.

"Dear Lord, I pray right now you touch this man's sperm and bring it to life. And touch his wife's eggs and bring them together in a holy collision of life and love."

I'm like, mental picture, mental picture, this is not happening!

And he prays for what seems like hours (it was probably just two minutes). And he looks at me and says, "It is done! It is done in the name of Jesus!"

I go, "Ain't quite done yet, Bob." Because faith without works is dead. And I don't think you can use the word sperm in a prayer.

I'm not kidding you, three weeks later—three weeks later—my wife got pregnant. We found out two months later, traced it back.

I sent him a postcard: "Dear Bob: It is done. Thanks for your prayer."

Bob and I may differ theologically, but let me tell you something. Bob prayed like God was standing there. And Bob prayed in faith.[12]

I would add, he prayed with bold imagination. He prayed with a vision of God doing something in the future that others might not have the eyes to see. But Bob did. And he prayed with a mental picture in mind—maybe too specific for Greg's comfort—of what God would do in answer to his prayer.

That's what Jesus intends for you and me to do when we pray. He tells us to "have faith in God." He tells us to speak to mountains. He tells us not to doubt in our hearts but to believe that what we pray will come to pass. And He says, "It will be yours."[13]

Pray with the attitude recommended by hymn writer Charles Wesley:

Faith, mighty faith, the promise sees,
And looks to that alone;

Laughs at impossibilities,
And cries, It shall be done![14]

Mighty God, give me boldness in prayer.
Teach me to pray mountain-moving prayers.
Teach me to pray in faith, knowing You to be a
dream-giving,
water-parting,
sun-stopping,
fire-sending,
giant-defeating,
exile-returning,
sickness-healing,
prisoner-freeing,
dead-raising,
prayer-answering God.
Teach me to pray big,
desperate,
heartfelt,
crumb-claiming,
will-not-take-no-for-an-answer prayers.
Teach me to pray imaginative,
creative,
visionary,
future-seeing,
future-changing prayers
that say, "It is done."
In Jesus' name, amen.

ENDNOTES

Diligent efforts have been made to identify, locate, and contact copyright holders and to secure permission to use copyrighted material. If any permsissions or acknowledgments have been inadvertently omitted or if such permission were not received by the time of publication, the publisher would sencerely appreciate receceiving complete information so that the correct credit can be gine in future editions.

Chapter 1: The Riches of the Red Letter Prayer Life
1. Ecclesiastes 9:7–10 MSG.
2. Matthew 7:18 ESV.
3. Basil Wood, "Hail, Thou Source of Every Blessing," public domain.
4. Psalm 1:1–3 ESV.
5. Numbers 24:6–7 CEB.
6. Jeremiah 17:7–8 ESV.
7. John 14:27 ESV.
8. Luke 10:19 ESV.
9. John 14:12 NLT.
10. See Hebrews 4:15.
11. Matthew 16:19 ESV.
12. Mark 1:35 ESV.
13. Mark 6:46 ESV.
14. Luke 5:16 NLT.
15. Luke 6:12 MSG.
16. Luke 9:18 ESV.
17. Luke 22:41 ESV.
18. Luke 11:1 ESV.
19. John Chrysostom, quoted in *Select Passages of the Writings of St. Chrysostom, St. Gregory Nazianzen, and St. Basil*, translated from the Greek by Hugh Stuart Boyd (London: Longman, Hurst, Rees, Orne and Brown, 1813), 26–27.
20. E. M. Bounds, *Purpose in Prayer* (Grand Rapids: Revell, 1920), 96.
21. Andrew Murray, *Lord, Teach Us to Pray* (Philadelphia: Henry Altemus, 1896), n.p.

Chapter 2: Pray Privately
1. Luke 11:1 ESV.
2. The Hebrew word means, literally, "repetition."
3. Matthew 6:5–6 ESV.

4. Matthew 6:5 ESV.
5. Deuteronomy 6:5 ESV.
6. See Psalm 55:17.
7. Matthew 6:5 ESV.
8. James Mulholland, *Praying Like Jesus* (San Francisco: HarperCollins, 2001), 15–16.
9. Anne Lamott, *Help Thanks Wow* (New York: Penguin Random House, 2012), 1. Used by permission.
10. Matthew 6:6 ESV.
11. Matthew 18:19 ESV.
12. N. T. Wright, *Matthew for Everyone: Part 1* (Louisville: Westminster John Knox, 2004), 56. Used by permission.
13. Mark 1:35 ESV.
14. Mark 6:46 ESV.
15. Luke 5:16 NLT.
16. Matthew 6:6 MSG.
17. Matthew 6:6 ESV.
18. Matthew 6:5 ESV.
19. Andrew Murray, *Lord, Teach Us to Pray* (Philadelphia: Henry Altemus, 1896), n.p.
20. Samuel Logan Brengle, *Helps to Holiness* (London: Salvationist Publishing, 1955), 40.

Chapter 3: Pray Simply
1. Matthew 6:7–8 ESV.
2. James Montgomery, "Prayer Is the Soul's Sincere Desire," public domain.
3. Matthew 6:8 ESV.
4. Richard Foster, *Prayer: Finding the Heart's True Home* (San Francisco: HarperSanFrancisco, 1992), 7–8.
5. Quoted in John Ortberg, *The Life You've Always Wanted* (Grand Rapids: Zondervan, 2002), 90.
6. Quoted in *Devotional Classics*, ed. Richard Foster and James Bryan Smith (San Francisco: HarperSanFrancisco, 1993), 138.
7. Luke 18:10–14 NLT.
8. 1 Kings 18:23–24 MSG.
9. 1 Kings 18:26–29 MSG.
10. Matthew 6:7 NIV.
11. 1 Kings 18:30–39 MSG.
12. Foster, *Prayer: Finding the Heart's True Home*, 8.
13. Peter Kreeft, *Prayer for Beginners* (San Francisco, CA: Ignatius Press, 2000), 33. Used by permission.
14. Gary Egeberg, *The Pocket Guide to Prayer* (Minneapolis, MN: Augsburg Fortress, 1999), 96.

15. Kreeft, *Prayer for Beginners*, 33.
16. 1 Samuel 3:10 NLT.
17. Robert Benson, *Living Prayer* (New York: Tarcher/Putnam, 1998), 134.
18. Matthew 6:7–8 ESV.
19. Foster, *Prayer: Finding The Heart's True Home*, 9.
20. Ephesians 6:18 NIV.
21. Philippians 4:6 NIV.
22. Matthew 7:7 MSG.

Chapter 4: Pray Communally
1. Samuel Coleridge, "The Ancient Mariner," *Poems* (London: J. M. Dent & Sons, 1974), 179.
2. Matthew 6:9–13 CJB.
3. John 14:13 ESV.
4. John 14:14 ESV.
5. John 16:23–24 ESV.
6. Hebrews 7:25 NLT.
7. Andrew Murray, *With Christ in the School of Prayer* (New Kensington, PA: Whitaker House, 1981), 195.
8. Romans 8:26–27 ESV.
9. Matthew 18:18–20 ESV.
10. John 17:11, 20–23 ESV, emphasis added.
11. Peter Tze Ming Ng, "Toward a New Agenda for Religious Education in a Multicultural Society," *Religious Education* 88, no. 4 (Fall 1993): 63–64.
12. Quoted in E. M. Bounds, *The Essentials of Prayer* (Grand Rapids: Baker Book House, 1979), 111.
13. Scot McKnight, *Praying with the Church: Following Jesus, Daily, Hourly, Today* (Brewster, MA: Paraclete Press, 2006), 11. Used by permission. www.paracletepress.com.
14. Murray, *With Christ in the School of Prayer*, 114.
15. Romans 8:26 ESV.
16. Romans 8:19–23 NLT.
17. N. T. Wright, *The Lord and His Prayer* (Grand Rapids: Eerdmans, 1997), 76. Used by permission.
18. James Mulholland, *Praying Like Jesus* (San Francisco: HarperSanFrancisco, 2001), 41.

Chapter 5: Pray Relationally
1. See John 5:18; 10:22–33.
2. These phrases are largely from the *Amidah* (also called the *Shemoneh Esrei*), the eighteen blessings that are a part of the daily prayers in Judaism. These prayers probably originated from around the time of Jesus or slightly after. While several prayers in the *Amidah* and other

Jewish prayers refer to God as Father, phrases such as those listed are predominant.
3. Luke 11:2 ESV.
4. Andrew Murray, *Lord, Teach Us to Pray* (Philadelphia: Henry Altemus, 1896), n.p.
5. Quoted in Larry Crabb, *The Papa Prayer* (Nashville: Integrity, 2006), 30. Used by permission.
6. Priscilla Brandt, *Two-Way Prayer* (Waco, TX: Word Books, 1979), 62–63.
7. N. T. Wright, *The Lord and His Prayer* (Grand Rapids: Eerdmans, 1997), 12. Used by permission.
8. Romans 8:15 NLT.
9. Galatians 4:6 NLT.
10. Crabb, *Papa Prayer*, 32.
11. Murray, *Lord, Teach Us to Pray.*
12. Wright, *The Lord and His Prayer*, 18–20.

Chapter 6: Pray Confidently
1. Matthew 6:9.
2. Exodus 3:7–8 ESV.
3. Deuteronomy 31:6 ESV.
4. Psalm 11:4 NIV.
5. Psalm 34:15 NLT.
6. 1 Peter 5:7 NIV.
7. See Psalm 121:4.
8. See Psalm 121:5–8.
9. Psalm 102:12, 25–28 ESV.
10. Isaiah 54:10 NIV.
11. Psalm 103:8–13 ESV.
12. N. T. Wright, *Surprised by Hope* (San Francisco: HarperOne, 2008), 115–16. Used by permission.
13. Ibid, 250.
14. Psalm 139:1–10 NLT.
15. Bill Hybels, *Too Busy Not to Pray* (Downers Grove, IL: InterVarsity Press, 1988), 29. Used by permission.
16. See Romans 4:21.
17. 2 Corinthians 9:8 NIV.
18. Luke 1:37 NIV.
19. Matthew 19:26 NIV.
20. See Jeremiah 32:17.
21. 2 Corinthians 9:8 NIV, emphasis added.
22. Hybels, *Too Busy Not to Pray*, 37.
23. E. M. Bounds, *The Possibilities of Prayer* (Grand Rapids: Baker Book House, 1979), 96–97.
24. Parts of this prayer are based on "The Magnificat," the prayer of Mary found in Luke 1:46–55, and on 2 Corinthians 9:8.

Chapter 7: Pray Cooperatively

1. Matthew 6:9–10 CJB.
2. Matthew 6:9–10 KJV.
3. Andrew Murray, *Lord, Teach Us to Pray* (Philadelphia: Henry Altemus, 1896), n.p.
4. Samuel Logan Brengle, *Take Time to Be Holy* (Wheaton, IL: Tyndale House Publishers, 2013), 323.
5. See Hayim H. Donin, *To Pray as a Jew: A Guide to the Prayer Book and the Synagogue Service* (New York: Basic Books, 1991), 80.
6. Philip Keller, *A Layman Looks at the Lord's Prayer* (Chicago: Moody Publishers, 1976), 49.
7. Numbers 20:12 ESV.
8. Leviticus 22:31–32 ESV.
9. 2 Samuel 6:20–22 GNT.
10. Nehemiah 8:10.
11. 2 Corinthians 6:10 NIV.
12. Matthew 13:44–46.
13. Matthew 13:33.
14. Matthew 13:31–32.
15. Luke 17:21.
16. Frederick Buechner, *Wishful Thinking: A Theological ABC* (New York: Harper & Row, 1973), 49–50.
17. N. T. Wright, *The Lord and His Prayer* (Grand Rapids: Eerdmans, 1997), 29. Used by permission.
18. Isaiah 6:8 KJV.
19. Keller, *Layman Looks at Lord's Prayer*, 63–64.
20. Murray, *Lord, Teach Us to Pray*, n.p.
21. Reginald Heber, "Holy, Holy, Holy," public domain.
22. Revelation 5:12 NIV.
23. Matthew 26:39 NIV.
24. Matthew 26:42 NIV.
25. Philippians 2:8 NIV.
26. Quoted in David Jeremiah, *Signs of Life: Back to the Basics of Authentic Christianity* (Nashville: Thomas Nelson, 2007), 31. Used by permission. All rights reserved.
27. Hebrews 12:22 NIV.
28. Keller, *Layman Looks at Lord's Prayer*, 49.
29. John 7:38.
30. See Habakkuk 2:14.

Chapter 8: Pray Practically

1. Used with permission.
2. Matthew 6:11 NIV.
3. Matthew 6:11 NIV.

4. Luke 11:1 NIV.
5. Luke 11:3 NIV.
6. Deuteronomy 8:10–14, 17–18 NIV.
7. Deuteronomy 8:17 NIV.
8. http://www.oneprayeraday.com
9. James 4:2–3 CJB.
10. Matthew 6:33 ESV.
11. Richard Andersen, *Living the Lord's Prayer* (St. Louis, MO: Concordia, 1994), 84–85.
12. See Genesis 1:5.
13. Mark 1:35 NIV.
14. Luke 4:42 NIV.
15. Psalm 55:17 ESV.
16. Daniel 6:10 ESV.
17. Anne Lamott, "Time Lost and Found," *Sunset* 224, no. 4 (April 2010), http://www.sunset.com/travel/anne-lamott-how-to-find-time. Used by permission.
18. Matthew 6:33 ESV.
19. Josiah Conder, "Day by Day the Manna Fell," public domain.
20. N. T. Wright, *The Lord and His Prayer* (Grand Rapids: Eerdmans, 1997), 45. Used by permission.
21. James Mulholland, *Praying Like Jesus* (San Francisco: HarperSanFrancisco, 2001), 82–83.

Chapter 9: Pray Specifically
1. Based on Mark 10:46–52.
2. Samuel Logan Brengle, *The Soul-Winner's Secret* (London: Salvationist, 1903), 12.
3. Matthew 6:11 KJV.
4. N. T. Wright, *The Lord and His Prayer* (Grand Rapids: Eerdmans, 1997), 44–45. Used by permission.
5. Andrew Murray, *With Christ in the School of Prayer* (New Kensington, PA: Whitaker House, 1981), 74.
6. James 1:17 NIV.
7. Wright, *The Lord and His Prayer*, 44–45.
8. Murray, *With Christ in the School of Prayer*, 75.
9. Psalm 38:9 NCV.
10. Charles Haddon Spurgeon, *The Treasury of David* (Peabody, MA: Hendrickson, 1990), 200.
11. Murray, *With Christ in the School of Prayer*, 75.
12. Philippians 4:19 KJV.
13. James 4:2 ESV.
14. See James 4:3.
15. Genesis 4:13–14.

16. Genesis 15:2
17. 1 Kings 19:4.
18. 2 Kings 20:3.
19. Psalm 18.
20. Habakkuk 1:2–4.
21. Judges 15:18.
22. 1 Samuel 1:10.
23. Luke 22:43.
24. C. S. Lewis, *Letters to Malcolm: Chiefly on Prayer* (New York: Harcourt, Brace, & World, 1964), 22.

Chapter 10: Pray Contritely
1. Matthew 6:9, 12 NLT.
2. Isaiah 57:15 NIV.
3. Luke 18:13–14 NIV.
4. Luke 8:13 ESV.
5. Karl Barth, *Prayer* (Louisville, KY: Westminster John Knox, 2002), 53. Used by permission.
6. Bill Hybels, *Too Busy Not to Pray* (Downers Grove, IL: InterVarsity Press, 1988), 53. Used by permission.
7. Ibid., 53–54.
8. Roger L. Ray, *Christian Wisdom for Today: Three Classic Stages of Spirituality* (Atlanta: Chalice Press, 1999), 39. Used by permission.
9. 1 John 1:9 ESV.
10. Philip W. Keller, *A Layman Looks at the Lord's Prayer* (Chicago: Moody Press, 1976), 116–17. Used by permission.
11. Albert Orsborn, "When Shall I Come unto the Healing Waters," The Salvation Army Songbook.
12. Hebrews 12:1 KJV.
13. William Shakespeare, *Hamlet*, act 3, scene 4, lines 149–50, 165–70.
14. Matthew 6:9 NLT.
15. Based on Albert Orsborn's "When Shall I Come unto the Healing Waters," The Salvation Army Songbook.

Chapter 11: Pray Graciously
1. Luke 11:4 GWT.
2. Matthew 6:11–12 ESV.
3. Matthew 6:14–15 ESV.
4. Matthew 18:23–35 ESV.
5. James Mulholland, *Praying Like Jesus* (San Francisco: HarperSanFrancisco, 2001), 104.
6. Compare the confession the prodigal practiced (in Luke 15:17–19) with the actual speech he delivered (in Luke 15:21), and you'll see that the father never gave his son the chance to finish his confession before showering him with mercy, kindness, and grace!

7. Colossians 3:13 NIV.
8. Matthew 18:25 ESV.
9. Matthew 18:26–27 ESV.

Chapter 12: Pray Submissively
1. Matthew 6:9–10 NKJV.
2. Matthew 6:11–13 ESV.
3. Exodus 16:12 ESV.
4. See Numbers 21:4–9.
5. Psalm 139:24 NLT.
6. Psalm 5:8 NLT.
7. Psalm 25:5 ESV.
8. Psalm 61:2 ESV.
9. Psalm 143:10 ESV.
10. Joseph Gilmore, "He Leadeth Me," public domain.
11. Matthew 4:1 ESV.
12. Mark 14:38 ESV.
13. Philip Keller, *A Layman Looks at the Lord's Prayer* (Chicago: Moody Publishers, 1976), 128. Used by permission.
14. Matthew 6:13 ESV.
15. Luke 22:28 ESV.
16. Luke 22:39–43 ESV.
17. See Matthew 26:36–46.
18. Romans 12:2 ESV.
19. N. T. Wright, *The Lord and His Prayer* (Grand Rapids: Eerdmans, 1997), 73–74. Used by permission.
20. Joseph Gilmore, "He Leadeth Me," public domain.
21. Luke 22:31–32 NIV.
22. Matthew 26:41 ESV.
23. Matthew 26:56 ESV.
24. Luke 23:46 ESV.
25. Joseph Gilmore, "He Leadeth Me," public domain.
26. Psalm 139:24 NLT.
27. Psalm 5:8 NLT.
28. Psalm 25:5 ESV.
29. Psalm 61:2 ESV.
30. Psalm 143:10 ESV.

Chapter 13: Pray Purposefully
1. Philip Keller, *A Layman Looks at the Lord's Prayer* (Chicago: Moody Publishers, 1976), 138. Used by permission.
2. Aleksandr Isaevich Solzhenitsyn, *The Gulag Archipelago, 1918–1956: Part 1* (New York: Harper & Row, 1973), 168.
3. Romans 7:15, 18–19, 21–25 ESV.

4. Romans 7:21 ESV.
5. Zechariah 3:2 ESV.
6. Adam Clarke, *Matthew to the Acts. Vol.5, Clarke's Commentary* (New York: Abingdon-Cokesbury, n.d.), 88.
7. In fact, some Bible versions translate this petition, "Deliver us from the evil one."
8. 1 Peter 5:8 ESV.
9. Robert Benson, *Living Prayer* (New York: Jeremy T. Parcher/Putnam, 1998), 131.
10. Ephesians 6:18 ESV.
11. St. Cyprian, quoted in Scott Hahn, *Understanding "Our Father"* (Steubenville, OH: Emmaus Road Publishing, 2002), 100.
12. Romans 7:21 ESV.
13. In fact, some Bible versions translate this petition, "Deliver us from the evil one."
14. 1 Peter 5:8 ESV.

Chapter 14: Pray Worshipfully

1. Seinfeld, "The Label Maker," season 6, episode 12 (https://www.youtube.com/watch?v=6WSD6Y2YWj4).
2. Rick Warren, *The Purpose-Driven Life* (Grand Rapids: Zondervan, 2002), 64. Used by permission of Zondervan. www.zondervan.com.
3. Matthew 6:13 KJV.
4. 1 Chronicles 29:11 NKJV.
5. N. T. Wright, *The Lord and His Prayer* (Grand Rapids: Eerdmans, 1997), 81. Used by permission.
6. Matthew 6:9–10 CJB.
7. Matthew 6:13 CJB.
8. Matthew 3:2 ESV.
9. Revelation 11:15 ESV.
10. Quotations are taken from Matthew 8:6–13 ESV.
11. Matthew 6:10 ESV.
12. Matthew 8:8 ESV.
13. Luke 22:42 NIV.
14. Matthew 26:39 ESV.
15. Psalm 40:8 ESV.
16. 1 Chronicles 29:11 ESV.

Chapter 15: Pray Gratefully

1. E. M. Bounds, *The Essentials of Prayer* (Grand Rapids: Baker Book House, 1979), 43.
2. John 11:38–44 ESV.
3. Colossians 1:16 ESV.
4. Matthew 11:3 NLT.

5. Matthew 11:11 NLT.
6. Matthew 11:20 ESV.
7. Matthew 11:25–26 ESV.
8. 1 Thessalonians 5:18 ESV.
9. 1 Thessalonians 5:18 MSG.
10. Matthew 5:16 NIV.
11. 1 Thessalonians 5:18 MSG.
12. Luke 24:30–31 ESV.
13. Anne Lamott, *Help Thanks Wow* (New York: Penguin Random House, 2012), 46–47.
14. 1 Thessalonians 5:18 ESV.

Chapter 16: Pray Biblically

1. Job 26:14 NLT (1996).
2. Job 26:14, margin, *The Prayer Bible*, ed. Jean E. Syswerda (Wheaton, IL: Tyndale House Publishers, 2003), 687. Used by permission.
3. Psalm 142:3 NLT (1996).
4. Psalm 142:3, margin, *Prayer Bible*, 832.
5. Ezekiel 37:5, margin, *Prayer Bible*, 1087.
6. Daniel 6:20–22, margin, *Prayer Bible*, 1117.
7. Malachi 4:2 NLT (1996).
8. Malachi 4:2, margin, *Prayer Bible*, 1214.
9. Deuteronomy 8:3 ESV.
10. Deuteronomy 6:16 ESV.
11. Matthew 4:10 NIV.
12. Matthew 27:46 ESV.
13. Psalm 22:6–8, 14–18, 23–24, 27 ESV.
14. Luke 23:46 ESV.
15. Psalm 31:5 NIV.
16. Matthew 27:46; Matthew 27:50; Mark 15:34; Luke 23:46.
17. Scot McKnight, *Praying with the Church: Following Jesus, Daily, Hourly, Today* (Brewster, MA: Paraclete Press, 2006), 54. Used by permission. www.paracletepress.com.
18. Jonah 2:1–9 NIV.
19. Psalm 27:1 ESV.
20. Psalm 42:11 ESV.
21. Eugene Peterson, *Answering God* (San Francisco: HarperSanFrancisco, 1989), 113. Used by permission.
22. Matthew 26:39 ESV.
23. Ephesians 3:14–21 ESV.
24. Colossians 1:9–12 ESV.

25. Charles G. Finney, *Principles of Prayer*, ed. Louis Parkhurst Jr. (Minneapolis: Bethany House, 2001), 47. Used by permission.

26. Ibid.

27. Bob Hostetler, *Quit Going to Church* (Abilene, TX: Leafwood, 2012), 54–55. Used by permission of Leafwood Publishers, an imprint of Abilene Christian University Press.

28. Wesley and Stacey Campbell, *Praying the Bible: The Pathway to Spirituality* (Ventura, CA: Regal Books, 2003), 155–56. Used by permission.

29. Psalm 19:6–14 MSG (slightly revised for praying).

Chapter 17: Pray Persistently

1. Mark Sheldon, "Jumbo's Journey to Majors Culminates in Cincinnati," June 20, 2014, http://m.mlb.com/news/article/80747322/jumbo-diazs-journey-to-majors-culminates-with-cincinnati-reds.

2. Andrew Murray, *With Christ in the School of Prayer* (New Kensington, PA: Whitaker House, 1981), 119. Used by permission.

3. Peter Kreeft, *Prayer for Beginners* (San Francisco: Ignatius Press, 2000), 124. Used by permission.

4. Luke 18:1 ESV.

5. Luke 11:5–9 ESV.

6. William Barclay, *The Daily Bible Study Series: The Gospel of Matthew* (Philadelphia: Westminster Press, 1975), 272.

7. Luke 18:1 NIV.

8. Luke 18:2–8 MSG.

9. Luke 11:9 NLT.

10. Luke 18:8 MSG.

11. Andrew Murray, *With Christ in the School of Prayer* (New Kensington, PA: Whitaker House, 1981), 122. Used by permission.

12. See Luke 9:51–55.

13. E. M. Bounds, *Purpose in Prayer* (Grand Rapids: Baker Book House, 1978), 58.

14. Genesis 32:24 ESV.

15. Genesis 32:26 ESV.

16. N. T. Wright, *Matthew for Everyone: Part 1* (Louisville: Westminster John Knox, 2004), 73. Used by permission.

Chapter 18: Pray Boldly

1. Matthew 7:7–11 NLT.

2. Mark 11:13 ESV.

3. Mark 11:14 ESV.

4. Mark 11:22–24 ESV.

5. When Jesus spoke of "this mountain" (Mark 11:23 ESV), He was probably referring to either Mount Zion, where the temple stood (see Mark 11:15–19) and which they could probably see, or the Mount of Olives, on which they probably stood.

6. Hebrews 4:16 KJV.

7. John 14:12–13 ESV.

8. Samuel Logan Brengle, *Take Time to Be Holy* (Wheaton, IL: Tyndale House Publishers, 2013), 216. Used by permission.

9. Hebrews 4:16 KJV.

10. Mark 11:22–23 ESV.

11. See http://www.dare2share.org/.

12. Transcribed from http://youthdownsouth.org/equip-2014-general-session-videos/; used with permission.

13. Mark 11:22–24 ESV.

14. Charles Wesley, "Father of Jesus Christ, My Lord," public domain.